Our creation was based on the modest notion that a professional basketball league might provide additional dates for arena operators to complete their winter schedules. Widespread public acceptance was slow in coming and economic success was elusive. But the game itself was nurtured by the collective passion of those who played, managed, attended, listened and watched. We became successful, first in the United States and then on a global basis. *The NBA at 50* gives us the opportunity to reminisce about our beginning, our development and a chance to celebrate the extraordinary contributions of those who have made our success possible.

David J. Stern

David J. Stern became the NBA's fourth commissioner in 1984.

THE NBA

AT FIFTY

Maurice Podoloff
1946-1963

J. Walter Kennedy
1963-1975

Larry O'Brien
1975-1984

This 1996 edition is published by Park Lane Press, a division of
Random House Value Publishing, Inc., 40 Engelhard Avenue,
Avenel, New Jersey 07001.

Park Lane Press and colophon are trademarks of
Random House Value Publishing, Inc.

Random House
New York • Toronto • London • Sydney • Auckland
http://www.randomhouse.com

Printed and bound in the United States of America

Library of Congress Cataloging-in-Publication Data

The NBA at 50 / edited by Mark Vancil.
                              p.   cm.
ISBN 0-517-20055-4 (hardcover : alk. paper); 0-517-20094-5 (trade paperback)
1. National Basketball Association—History. 2. National Basketball Association—
Pictorial works. I. Vancil, Mark, 1958-.
GV885.515.N37N32   1996

Produced by:
Rare Air, Ltd.
A Mark Vancil Company
130 Washington Street
West Dundee, IL 60118

Designed by:
John Vieceli
McMillan Associates

*For my wife, Laura; my grandmother, Mary Kathryn Mabel;
my mother, Jacqueline Vancil and my sisters, Susan and Jane.
The best of me comes from them.*

MLV 1996

Voters for the 50 Greatest Players of the First 50 Years.
The 50 Greatest Players can be found beginning on page 76.

Abdul-Jabbar, Kareem
Albert, Marv
Attles, Al
Auerbach, Red
Baylor, Elgin
Bing, Dave
Bird, Larry
Blake, Marty
Blinebury, Fran
Bill
Brown, Hubie
Chamberlain, Wilt
Chernoff, Mitch
Cousy, Bob
Cunningham, Billy
Daly, Chuck
DuPree, David

Embry, Wayne
Erving, Julius
Gilmartin, Joe
Goldaper, Sam
Hannum, Alex
Harrison, Lester
Havlicek, John
Hearn, Chick
Holzman, Red
Jasner, Phil
Johnson, Earvin "Magic"
Kerr, John
Koppett, Leonard
Lanier, Bob
Layden, Frank
Lewin, Leonard
McCallum, Jack

McGuire, Dick
Mikan, George
Pettit, Bob
Pollack, Harvey
Ramsay, Jack
Reed, Willis
Robertson, Oscar
Russell, Bill
Ryan, Bob
Schayes, Dolph
Sharman, Bill
Shue, Gene
Thomas, Isiah
Unseld, Wes
Vecsey, Peter
West, Jerry

ACKNOWLEDGMENTS

If the essence of a team is the selfless contribution to a common goal, then this book is the physical embodiment of that concept. From the first conceptual meetings on through to the long series of late nights and early mornings, individuals from every corner of the NBA, Random House and our partners and friends at McMillan Associates never once failed to come through. Though there were countless contributions, including those of World Color, specifically Jim Forni and Christy Egan, the following went above and beyond any reasonable expectation.

At the outset, Frank Fochetta's leadership and insight brought the many pieces of this project together and bridged the wide gap between concept and execution. At Random House, Bill Huelster's vision and drive moved us all forward while Judy Tropea's touch kept the project on track. At NBA Properties, the leadership of Rick Welts and Bill Daugherty, who organized an array of disparate groups on our behalf, was invaluable. So too was Diane Naughton who calmly manuevered behind the scenes. And at Communications, Brian McIntyre's support and unique ability remain much appreciated constants.

The entire process benefitted from the focus and insight provided by NBA Publishing Ventures, particularly Jan Hubbard, whose guidance and expertise smoothed the edges; Chris Ekstrand, who reviewed every name, number and nuance; and Alex Sachare who walked us through history.

The project was brought to life in large part thanks to Charlie Rosenzweig at NBA Photos and the uncommon commitment to excellence and service by Carmin Romanelli and his staff, particularly Eric Weinstein, Marc Hirschheimer and Joe Amati, all of whom never tired of our endless requests and always tried to find an even better shot. Thanks also to Adam Silver and Don Sperling at NBA Entertainment where Jim Podhoretz, Larry Weitzman and Steve Browning made sure we never ran out of sources. And to Rich Fried, whose late-night updates and overall focus never went unnoticed.

Still, we all would have been operating in the dark without the shining light that is Zelda Spoelstra. Her passion and dedication can be traced from the inception of the league on through to the pages of this book. Zelda's knowledge and spirit were enjoyed by all of us fortunate enough to work with her.

Finally, one more standing ovation for the attention to detail and unsurpassing commitment to excellence from our partners at McMillan Associates, particularly Michael McMillan, Anne McMillan and Jeanne Thomson, all of whom know more about the NBA than they ever thought possible, and John Vieceli, whose unique approach is matched only by his talent.

To one and all, our heartfelt appreciation.

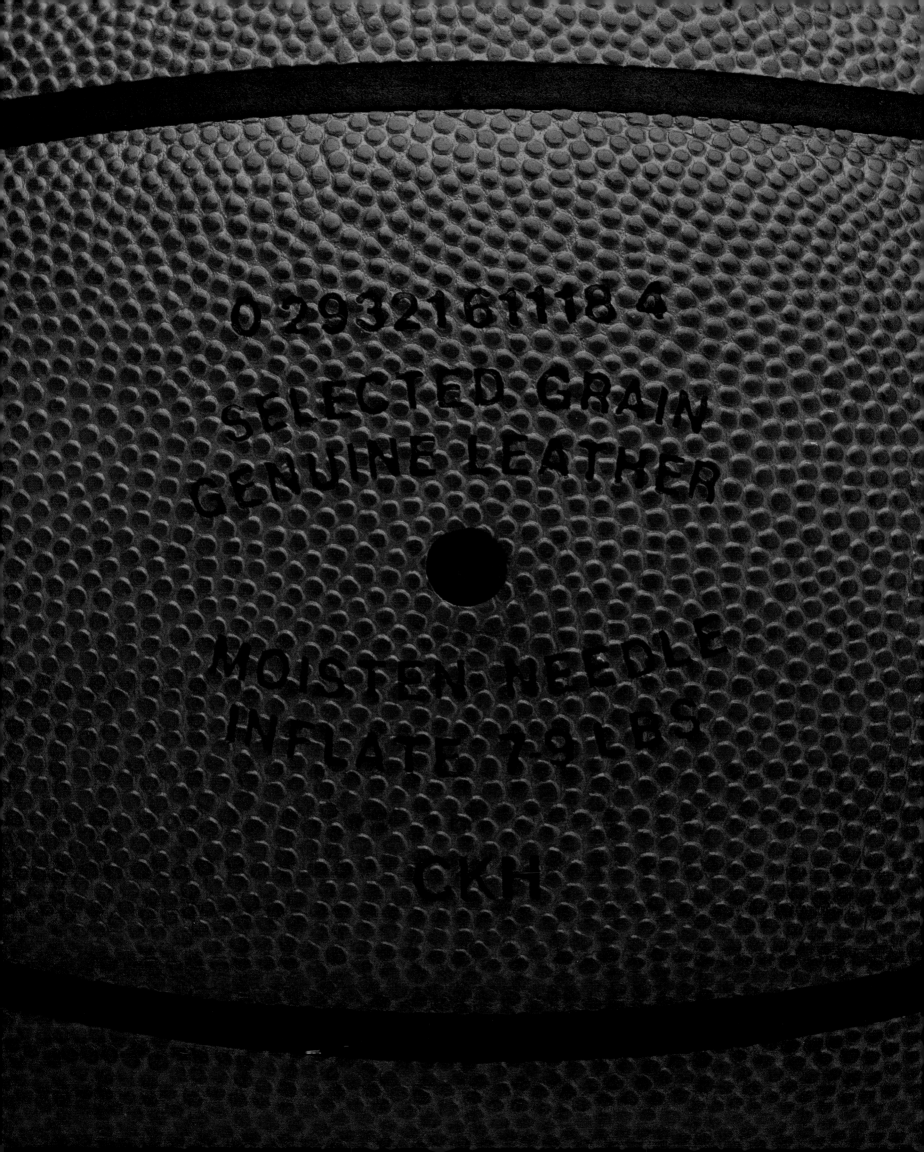

Contents

FOREWORD

by David Halberstam

It is early in June of 1996. The greatest and arguably the most captivating athlete that I have ever seen play in any sport in my lifetime is about to play in what is effectively a showdown game for him against a team from Seattle. The varying elevator and doormen who work in our building and the other buildings on our block on the West side of Manhattan, knowing that I occasionally write about professional basketball, want to talk to me about the player and the game. None of these men, to my knowledge, was born in the United States. They come from all over the world, the Dominican Republic, Panama, the Philippines, the Indian sub-continent. I doubt that any of these men played basketball as a boy, just as I doubt that many of them seriously watched a basketball game until he was well into his twenties. Yet he is "Michael" to them. No one refers to him by his last name. Their relationship is far too intimate for that. They root for him and for his team even though they are not from Chicago; indeed, I am not sure any of them has ever been to Chicago, or for that matter to Seattle.

But they know I have met and written about Michael Jordan and I am their connection to him. What happens now is fascinating: We communicate to each other, across the vast barriers of class, ethnicity, language and generations, through the instrument of Michael Jordan on the eve of a critical playoff game in the National

Michael Jordan, 1996 NBA Finals

Basketball Association. When so much else in our respective lives seems to separate us, he and the skill he plays with, are what we have in common. On this day, Game 6 of the Chicago-Seattle Finals, they not only want him to win, but they want him to win tonight, to end it all. They do not want him to let the series drag on, and thereby taint even slightly so astonishing a season for him and his teammates. They are committed to him: It is the most remarkable of commitments to a surpassing athlete in a sport they never played, in a country which is only now becoming theirs. They are upset that the Bulls have lost two in a row to Seattle. The first time was acceptable, the law of averages. "I always thought it would go five," says one of them, Ralph Thomas, an elevator operator originally from the Dominican Republic. The second time they believe, however, was inexcusable. There was a notable and unacceptable lack of concentration on the part of the Bulls. But they are confident about tonight's game — they believe Michael will play big in a big game in his own house, a phrase they have learned to use. They have faith in him; the bigger the game, one of them says, the bigger he plays.

It takes me back to memories from my boyhood. I am younger, and living in a suburb of New York, and the Yankees are in their annual cliffhanger of a pennant race, or have finally reached the World Series, and when this happens men and boys who might otherwise be strangers talk to each other about what Joe or, in this case, "DiMag" or DiMaggio, will do against assorted Red Sox, Brooklyn Dodger or St. Louis Cardinal pitchers. They referred, of course, to the great DiMaggio, the surpassing big game athlete who bound us together in my youth and whose deeds allowed strangers to find commonality and community with each other.

There are a number of things about this dramatic change in the world of sports that I find striking. The first is that basketball because of the stunning talents of its great athletes and the speed of the sport, has at the very least gained parity with baseball and football as a national spectator sport, at least among younger Americans. This is something that goes beyond mere rating points during the Finals, compared to the World Series or the Super Bowl. Rather it is something that has *happened* — it is the psyche of the nation, particularly among younger Americans; the deeper into the playoffs, the more schedules in all kinds of Americans' homes are set, according to the schedule dictated by the NBA for the games, so that a crucial big game not be missed.

Connie Hawkins

The second thing is that the most idolized and admired athletic hero in America, some fifty years after the color barrier was broken by Jackie Robinson, is a young, gifted black man, and that even Madison Avenue realizes this and that the proof is there in commercial endorsements — Michael Jordan is by far the greatest salesman of sneakers, underwear, soft drinks, breakfast foods, and above all himself and his sport, not just in America, but in the world today. Here in a country that until very recently has liked to think of itself as being white and where until very recently black athletes did not get anywhere near their share of commercial endorsements, he is not merely an athletic superstar, but a cultural icon who has given us a new and far broader definition of beauty.

And the third thing is that this sport, with the intensity of its play, and the physical beauty and balletic ability of its signature athletes, has become the hot sport in the modern era, when the competition among different forms of entertainment for viewer time is more intense every year. In a nation where the pace of life, driven by jet planes, by television, by computers and faxes and e-mail gets faster all the time, basketball seems to fit the changed national appetite, and supply the requisite amount of action in the limited amount of time people now have to watch. That is most notable during the playoffs, when the baseball season is just beginning and the basketball season is at its peak, and the pace of the two very different sports is so easy to compare. More, the quantum increase in the quality of the video equipment, the cameras on location, and the receivers in the home, catches not just the raw emotion of the players, but provides the spectator a great sense of intimacy with basketball's athletes, an intimacy not attainable in other sports.

The action of football is fast and brilliant, but its athletes wear all kinds of clunky armor and the men themselves therefore seem more distant. Baseball is slow, it is by and large not an adrenaline game, the emotions of its players, perhaps because of the traditional culture of the game, perhaps because if you celebrate too readily the pitcher may throw at you the next time up, are more often than not rather guarded. But basketball is played in a fury, offense to defense and back to offense again in micro seconds, and the emotions born of that ferocity cannot be hidden; the emotions are raw, and they are naked to the camera. It is, not surprisingly, the fastest growing sport in the world and the NBA game has become the signature of that growth; at the Olympics, it is the American stars from the NBA that all the other world-class athletes want to meet, pose for candid photo shots with, and get autographs from. No other sport, it appears, lends itself so brilliantly to the modern era, to an audience that has all kinds of entertainment competing for its ever more limited attention span.

It is in our bloodstream now, and has been for some 15 years, since the Magic Johnson/Larry Bird, Los Angeles Lakers/Boston Celtics rivalry first flowered. The baseball season still starts in April, but in any real sense the baseball season now has to wait to catch the attention of the American sports fan until the NBA Finals are completed. Basketball, in no small part because of a handful of gifted and unusually winning athletes such as Jordan and Johnson, captivated the young at precisely the moment that the nation was ready to tune in. Recently, former governor Mario Cuomo of New York wondered aloud where all the American athletic heroes have gone — and wondered why today's youth did not seem to have heroes comparable to those of his own youth, like Joe DiMaggio and Ted Williams. A friend of mine named Dick Holbrooke, then a Wall Street broker, later the principal United States negotiator in Bosnia, wrote Cuomo that these heroes still exist, but that they played a different sport, basketball, and that their names were Magic Johnson, Larry Bird, and Michael Jordan. I stand corrected, Cuomo wrote him.

It was not always thus. The date was November 1, 1946. Harry Truman was the President, still greatly maligned, even by members of his own party, and regarded as a poor successor to the majestic Franklin Roosevelt. The Russians had not yet exploded an atomic bomb. The supply of automobiles being produced by Detroit still did not meet the demand of an America, with the war and the Depression finally over, that wanted to get out of its pre-war jalopies, and so customers had to slip car dealers money under the table in order to get to the head of the line and buy a new car. Out on Long Island a man named Bill Levitt was buying up potato farms and plowing them under, and erecting his own new village, to be called Levittown; returning veterans could buy a house from him for $7,000 (with a free dishwasher thrown in) with only $100 down.

But on November 1, basketball history was made without, of course, those who were making the history knowing that they were making it. It was the first game of a new basketball league then known as the Basketball Association of America, and soon to be known as the NBA, the National Basketball Association. It was played in Toronto between the Toronto Huskies and a new team called the New York Knickerbockers. Ossie Schectman, a former Long Island University star, made the first basket in the new league, good for two of the 11 points he was to score that night and of the 435 he was to score in that season, the only year he played. The Knicks won 68-66. Some 10,000 people showed up to watch the game. The Toronto star was Ed (Big Ed) Sadowsky who had played at Seton Hall. The appearance of Big Ed, who was all of 6-feet-5, and played center and scored 18 points, had been hyped before the game. "Here Comes The Huskies (Jet-Propelled)" an ad in the *Toronto Globe and Mail* said, and it showed Big Ed holding the ball. "Thrills — Spills — Action —

Earvin "Magic" Johnson

Speed," the ad also promised. Ticket prices ranged from 75 cents to $1.25, to $2.00 to $2.50. The Toronto fans, the Knicks players noted, were extremely gracious but not particularly hip, cheering politely for every goal, but clearly Canada was still hockey country, and they knew little about basketball. Every time there was a jump ball, someone would yell that there was going to be a face-off.

The first game in the old Madison Square Garden a few days later drew some 17,000 fans. Ned Irish, the owner of the Knicks was thrilled — he had hoped for 12,000 and this greatly exceeded his expectations. The Knick team was loaded up with former New York City athletes who had been great college stars at LIU, CCNY and NYU, and were therefore local favorites, this in a city where the sport was big time long before it became a big national draw. The fans were quite savvy and identified with their former college heroes. Bill Roeder, a sportswriter working for the *New York World Telegram*, wrote disapprovingly about the ticket prices ($5 top) but approvingly on the crowd response (the crowd "wildly howled the game into its extra period, their favor approaching NYU-Notre Dame capacity in decibel content."). The players were all white, and they still used the old-fashioned two-handed set shot. But the NBA was on its way. The idea that it might rival baseball for the nation's spotlight within the remaining part of the twentieth century, or that its most celebrated athletes would become greater cultural icons than those of baseball, seemed inconceivable.

Sonny Hertzberg, a 5-foot-10 forward on that team, a former star at CCNY, remembered the Garden debut with pleasure. In the past he had played for other pro teams but there had been a fly-by-night quality to it all, and he had been paid by the game, $50 or $75 a

Walt Frazier

shot. Ned Irish had signed him for $4,500 for the season, which was fairly good money then, and told him he did not need more because since he was an optician, he would be able to make even more money in the offseason. But the season was long, and there were playoff games as well, and Hertzberg was not able to work in the offseason. Instead, Irish gave him a $1,500 bonus at the end of the season (he had been the leading scorer on the Knicks with his terrific two-handed set shot) and with the additional $750 he made in playoff money, he earned nearly $7,000. But the money was not the thing, he recalls fifty years later: "I was like all the rest of our team and the players we played against — we loved the game. We would have played for nothing."

Hertzberg was thrilled to be a part of something as solid as the NBA, self-evidently more stable than other previous leagues because the owners, city by city, seemed to be the people who owned or managed the major arenas, such as the Garden or the Chicago Stadium. Because of that, there was a surprisingly solid feel to the league. There was a certain stability to having a contract, a certain glamour in going into different cities and playing in the biggest arena around. Each Knick player got one home uniform — white, and one blue road uniform. Making sure that they were clean or even semi-clean was the responsibility of the players themselves. The ownership provided socks and jocks. Hertzberg even got one commercial during his time with the Knicks for *Rise*, a shaving cream. He was paid $350. From the start there was one essential truth about the league: the athletes were good, the best of the college players, the product was good, the games were competitive. If the professional game had not yet created the tradition and rivalries of the college game, the quality of play was better. More, unlike most college teams where the best players all too quickly graduated, the NBA teams had continuity — the essential core of a team might hold together for six or seven years. That sense of continuity was vital to the early growth of the professional football league, and in time, to professional basketball as well.

The America it was born into fifty years ago was a very different country. No one in those days talked about the Entertainment Dollar. The men who ran professional sports teams thought they were sporting men, not entertainment men. The idea of broadening the appeal of your product, what later came to be known as marketing, was to hold Ladies Day in baseball once or twice a year. It was still a Calvinist America, the pursuit of pleasure and entertainment was a secondary impulse; the core of the economy was one where men, not women, went off to work every day wearing blue-collar shirts and carrying lunch buckets, and put in a long, hard day of physical labor. Women stayed at home, cooked and raised their children. No one questioned Dad's opinion at the dinner table. The country was white, or at least it thought of itself as still being white, and it operated in all its effective mechanisms, economic, social and political, as if it were completely white.

The pace of life was in comparison to today, leisurely. Television was just beginning to be broadcast in a handful of Eastern cities, in vague, often trembling black-and-white images, surrounded by shadows and ghosts. The music industry was relatively small and unimportant compared to today. The principal artists were men like Bing Crosby and Frank Sinatra who had the good sense to keep their hair well trimmed. If there were black entertainers, they either sang

Dominique Wilkins

in a white mode like Nat Cole, or they stayed within the assigned orbit of jazz. Nor was there such a thing as fast food, although in San Bernardino, California, two brothers named Dick and Maurice (Mac) McDonald were just learning how to streamline their roadside take-out food restaurant, getting rid of the barbecue and chicken dishes, and selling instead only hamburgers. As such, they began to mechanize the process much as Henry Ford had once mechanized the automobile assembly line. The result was a smashing success. They called their little place McDonald's.

Both transportation and communications moved at a much slower pace. There was no federally sponsored superhighway system yet, no such thing as FedEx. A web was something spiders wove; a net was something firemen and fishermen used. A commercial airplane flight across the country involved multiple stops. The main instrument of communications that informed and entertained Americans in their home was radio, which had been made infinitely more powerful and legitimate during the war years when it had permitted an anxious nation to follow the course of its warriors in Europe and the South Pacific.

The world of sports was narrowly circumscribed. The preeminent sport was baseball, a game with a pleasant leisurely pace; its slow tempo, the long moments between the quick bursts of action made it an ideal subject for transmission by radio. What ensued was a perfect marriage of sport and technology. Professional football existed and had its own passionate aficionados, but its place in the sports pantheon in the pre-television years was in all ways effectively minor league. As for pro basketball, well, there had been leagues before, but they had never captured the imagination of ordinary

Americans, never seeped into the bloodstream of the society.

Baseball in 1946 reflected more the country as it had been than the country as it was soon to be. The two leagues contained a total of 16 teams. Washington was considered a Southern city, St. Louis a Western one; there were no major league teams in California. The teams traveled by train, a factor that greatly limited geographic location. The owners held complete control over their players; their power in salary negotiations was nothing less than dictatorial. Not surprisingly, salaries, even for the superstar players in all sports, were quite low given the commercial box-office value of what they did.

The handful of signature players who had returned from the war, DiMaggio, Williams, Musial and Feller were edging towards the $100,000 figure. Journeymen players made between $5,000 and $7,000. Most players badly needed jobs in the off-season to sustain their lifestyle. The idea of a professional athlete working in the off-season in a weight room to build up his strength and to arrive at spring training in tiptop shape was essentially unheard of.

Most important of all, the faces were all still white, reflecting an American belief that this was still a white nation. That was about to end. In the summer of 1946, Branch Rickey had introduced his first black player, the carefully selected Jackie Robinson, into the team's AAA farm club in Montreal where he had made a sensational debut. The next year Robinson would break the color line in major league baseball; there, playing with a combination of fire and ice he would dazzle the world of baseball and become rookie of the year. More quietly, in the less scrutinized new upstart football league, the All-American Football Conference, an innovative man named Paul Brown had already signed and

Alex English (2)

suited two black players, the lineman John Wooten and the great running back Marion Motley.

But it was Robinson who changed not merely the world of sports but the country. He was nothing less than history's man. He turned sports into a central arena of what was to become the Civil Rights struggle. Fiery, talented, highly intelligent, he played like a black Ty Cobb; he not only brought in a new dimension of speed and power to the game, but in the process swept aside a century's worth of clichés with which white men had fortified themselves while denying black Americans full participation in American life.

Everywhere he played he made converts, many of them, it should be noted, extremely reluctant and trudging conversions. Baseball was at first the obvious beneficiary of his talents and the talents of those other great black athletes who came right after him, Willie Mays, Frank Robinson, Henry Aaron, Bob Gibson, Larry Doby. They brought speed and power to a slow game in a sleepy country. No one considered the possibility at the time, that the coming of these great athletes to other sports that might showcase their talents *better than baseball* might one day jeopardize the primacy of baseball.

But the country was changing and changing quickly. In the Fifties the nation turned to television. By 1952 there were 19 million television sets in American homes and 1,000 new stores selling television sets were opening up each month. By 1954, by some estimates, as many as 50 million people watched certain segments of the popular *I Love Lucy* show on television. A technological revolution was taking place, not only sweeping the country, but also changing it. That was to prove particularly true in the world of sports. If radio was comfortable with the leisurely pace of the past, then television was something new: It demanded action, action in its news (its newscasters and executive producers loved the accelerating Civil Rights struggle in the South, not just because it was a great moral crisis, but because it provided much needed action footage as well), action in its regular programs — cop shows and Westerns — and action in its sports.

That was just a part of a larger process that saw the pace of life in America grow ever faster. By the early Sixties, jet travel was becoming a part of the fabric of daily life, helping to open up California and Texas for demographic and economic expansion. Television changed the way Americans lived. Politicians — and this was to become true in sports as well — were no longer just politicians; they were also potentially stars. One of the things that catapulted the young and very junior John Kennedy ahead of his other Democratic rivals in 1960, and eventually ahead of Richard Nixon, was that he had star quality. More and more because of television, every aspect of our national life had to entertain us. Television, of course, profoundly affected the world of sports.

Sports was no longer just sports, it was surprisingly inexpensive mass-market entertainment. Probably the first person in sports who realized this was an old promoter/agent named Sonny Werblin who, putting together a football team called the New York Jets in a rival upstart league and knowing little about football, decided to sign a quarterback named Joe Namath over another potentially equally gifted rookie quarterback because meeting Namath for the first time, he was excited by his charisma and was convinced that he had

Kareem Abdul-Jabbar (33)

star quality. Then Werblin deliberately paid Namath more than he needed to, knowing that the very size of the contract would make him an even bigger star.

The explosion in sports happened first with football then basketball. In a stunningly short time professional football gained a psychic parity with baseball in the hearts of ordinary fans. The camera loved its action and the sheer ferocity of its play; the tempo seemed to fit the uses of television as radio had suited the pace of baseball. The decade of the Fifties had opened with one sport, baseball, dominating the national sports platform, and had ended with another, football, sharing it. In the world of television, if the product was good, if it was real, then the past and the tradition meant less and less, for a new rivalry could be instantly created and artificially hyped and orchestrated.

The same revolution took a decade longer with basketball. Back in the Forties it had not been a truly national game. Baseball had its roots in rural America, where there were plenty of green fields to play on and where rival villages played against each other on Saturdays and Sundays. Basketball's roots were very different. They were either in the cities where urban kids lacking baseball diamonds had played on concrete courts or on the streets themselves, or in rural villages where country kids who went to schools too small to field baseball or football teams practiced alone by the hour on primitive homemade courts. It had always lacked the comparable hold on the national consciousness of baseball and football. But the product was good and getting better. As the camera liked football because of the action, it liked basketball for the same reason and the camera work itself was getting better all the time. Not only did that mean that the fan sitting in his or her living room could enjoy the game more, but it meant that the fan was becoming more hip because the camera was a brilliant teacher. The country was beginning to learn the importance of defense, to understand the pick and roll, and to grasp that a truly great basketball player was not someone with exceptional stats, rather a truly great player was someone who made other players better.

The early years for the NBA remained relatively shaky, indeed. When the Boston Celtics in the mid-Fifties were short a man or two, a young man named Skip Whitaker, who had starred at Kentucky and who had chosen to go to Harvard Business School rather than to play pro ball, would dress for Celtic home games. He played in three Celtic games in 1955-56 for a total of 15 minutes, hit one of his six shots, committed one personal foul and had one assist. (You could, as Casey Stengel used to say, look it up.)

That same year when Tom Gola came to the Philadelphia Warriors from LaSalle, where over four years he had set the career college rebounding record (that he still holds), he had asked the Warriors owner, Eddie Gottlieb, for a salary of $17,000. Gottlieb said that was too much, he couldn't meet so grand a price. So Gottlieb cut a deal with Gola: He would pay him $15,000 and in addition he would give Gola a night in his honor at which he would receive a free car worth approximately $2,000. (Which Gola did, getting a new Dodge; years later he remembered that when Bob Pettit and Cliff Hagan had had their nights they had gotten the rather tonier *Oldsmobiles*). Nor did NBA salaries go up very quickly, particularly in Boston where Red Auerbach was clearly the league's smartest executive.

Tom "Satch" Sanders

When Satch Sanders graduated from NYU in 1960 he was uncertain whether or not his future lay with the NBA. After all, the previous year his teammate and close friend at NYU, Cal Ramsey, who had been an All-American and who had led the nation in rebounding, had been drafted by St. Louis. But the Hawks had quickly unloaded him and passed him on to New York. If Ramsey could not stick with the Hawks, thought Sanders, there was little hope for him in the pros. But the Celtics drafted him in the first round and Auerbach offered him all of $8,000 to play. Sanders had an offer on the table from an AAU team to play what was considered semi-pro ball with the Tuck Tapers. That might lead to a career position long after his basketball days were over.

The idea that he might take a job with the AAU team and turn down the Celtics appalled the noted economist Arnold Auerbach. *"The AAU!"* he shouted at Sanders as if in mortal pain, "Don't be crazy! Anyone can get a job! But we're talking about playing with the *Boston Celtics!"* Sanders' mother agreed with Auerbach and so he signed with the Celtics. (As a rookie, it was Sanders' job to play defense, to rebound, and to launder Bill Russell's jersey after every game when they were on the road.)

If Auerbach was tight with the team's money he was not that different from a number of the other early owner/general managers whose payroll money came from their own pockets. Typical of the old breed was Ben Kerner, the shrewd owner of the old St. Louis Hawks, who had signed the young Lenny Wilkens for a pittance, and then tried to keep his salary as low as possible, despite the fact that Wilkens was a perennial All-Star. At one point in his career Wilkens had edged his way up to $14,000. When it came time to sign his next contract, Wilkens found that he and Kerner could not easily reduce the gap between them. At one point it was only $2,000. They kept talking and narrowed it to $1,000. "Are you going to let $1,000 stand between us?" Kerner asked Wilkens. "No," said Wilkens. "Good," said Kerner handing him a contract, "sign here." And Lenny Wilkens had signed.

It was Auerbach, of course, more than any other man who helped shepherd the league into the modern era, created the prototype new definition of a professional team, and had the shrewdest eye for the emerging black talent just beginning to come out of America's colleges. He was in many ways the early visionary of the sport. He was far ahead of the curve in understanding how important defensive ability was in drafting black players when it was not yet fashionable, and in defying conventional racial taboos by playing five black players at a time.

For the players were getting bigger and more athletic and, to be honest, blacker all the time. The new American athletic talent bank more and more reflected one of the remarkable ironies of American society —

Bill Russell (6) and Oscar Robertson (14)

our best athletes were the descendants of slaves. They were, in the larger process of racial change taking place in the country, beginning to go to better schools and colleges, getting better coaching, and eating a better diet. Jackie Robinson had turned out to be a far more revolutionary figure than anyone had realized at the time. For if television was creating one revolution, then a second revolution was taking place in sports, where for the first time black athletes surged to their rightful place in American life. It was nothing less than a crucial part of the larger Civil Rights revolution that was exploding throughout the country, although the results were more dramatic in sports where the playing field was always more level than in the rest of life. It was in sports where generation old stereotypes — about what blacks could and could not do — collapsed more quickly.

In no sport, not even football, would the change be so dramatic as basketball, nor would it happen in so short a time. Arguably basketball surged into the big time and set its own new high standard of professionalism with the coming of Bill Russell to the league in 1956-57. He was the most dominant team athlete of the modern sports era — for the Celtics won 11 championships in the 13 years he played. No one had ever seen a big man so agile and so strong before, with such balletic ability. In his first professional game he got 21 rebounds in 16 minutes; a few days later in a game against the Warriors he held Neil Johnston, then one of the league's leading scorers, without a field goal for the first 42 minutes and gathered 18 rebounds of his own. As intelligent as he was physically gifted, he very simply changed the nature of the game; because he could play above the rim, the other players would have to, too. When three years later Wilt Chamberlain entered the league, another giant with comparable athletic ability, their rivalry and the rivalry of their two teams transcended the sport, and brought to it spectators who up until then were not necessarily basketball fans, but who in time became fans.

So it was in the Sixties that the sport gradually moved towards the big time. If it did not yet rival football or baseball, it was moving to a more central place in the ever expanding world of televised sports. As the definition on the television screen got better and better, so the fans seemed to be moving up to an ever better seat in the front row. That television was making it more attractive was reflected by the coming of a new, relatively well-financed, basketball league in 1967, the American Basketball Association. It played a wide open game, had a wacky looking multi-colored ball, and awarded three points for a long jump shot. It also had players who played with an electric quality above the rim that dazzled old-time NBA fans, even those who fancied themselves as purists.

Suddenly the floodgates were open: In 1966 there were five black and five white players taken in the first round of the NBA Draft; in 1967, for the first time of the 12 players chosen, a majority, eight, were black. The average sports fan was becoming more and more aware of the sheer, almost magical ability of these great athletes — the fact that they did not merely run and jump, but there was something artistic to their flight. They had what came to be called "moves." The blacks themselves had always known about it. They had seen the moves on the playgrounds, but now, for the first time, they were showing them on national television. The first player to dent the national consciousness with his agility and power and his moves was probably Elgin Baylor. And after him there was Connie Hawkins, and then eventually Julius Erving and finally Michael Jordan.

If anything, the game was probably ahead of the country for a time, perhaps blacker than some traditional fans were willing to accept, particularly sports fans who had grown up in the Thirties, Forties and Fifties, and equally important, blacker than the taste-making advertising executives, who had grown up in those years and

Julius Erving

retained the prejudices of their childhood, were comfortable with. But gradually there was an awareness that the action was compelling, and with the arrival of younger and younger fans, traditional prejudices began to soften. The game seemed to blend in more readily with the pace of modern life and to appeal to a generation less burdened by race, and more anxious to fill its leisure time with ever faster action. Because the NBA was the least rooted of the three sports, it constantly adjusted its rules in order to speed up the action and at the same time to showcase its remarkable athletes. That started with the 24-second clock, which ended any ability of slower, less talented players to kill the clock (and the game), and it has continued with constant adjustments, some smaller, some larger, over the years. If the big men were becoming too big and too rough and the action around the basket was becoming too physical, the league knew when to open things up by adopting the three-point shot.

The matching of the game to the speed of the modern era, was as commissioner David Stern has noted, almost involuntary. The result, he has noted, is that "our game ended up being better suited to the contemporary pace of life today. The MTV generation wants action — these young people demand life at a faster pace, they want their news faster, their entertainment faster, their pizza delivered faster. They are raised on fast foods and fast sports. And we are there delivering a lot of action in a short span of time." Nothing reflected the speed and the intensity of the NBA more than a playoff game in 1995 between the Orlando Magic and the Indiana Pacers where the lead changed hands four times in the final 14 seconds.

Baseball remained a beautiful sport, but it was the cumulative sense of the game, and the exterior intensity mandated by a pennant race which worked for the sport. For a very long time it had little competition and it had fans, though in their forties and fifties, whose childhoods were rooted in a time when baseball was the dominating sport. It drew as much on memory as it did on its own competitive position. The action itself rarely had the intensity of a high-level basketball game. Nor was baseball a particularly good place to showcase a great athlete. The talents it demanded were highly specialized, the ability to hit a breaking ball thrown at 90 miles an hour, rather than broad-gauged.

By contrast no other sport showcased the fullness of the ability of the great modern black athlete so completely as basketball, that combination of speed and power and agility and intelligence. Ironically, nearly five years after Jackie Robinson broke into baseball it was the weakest platform among the three major sports for the athletes who were his lineal descendants. Even if Michael Jordan, in his brief sabbatical into professional baseball, had been more successful, even if he could have shown that he could hit a curve ball, he would never have been as exciting a baseball player as he is a basketball player; the confines of the sport do not permit it. In football a gifted quarterback throws the ball, a great wide receiver might break free and catch it, but the roles are more limited, the talents broken down into more highly specialized slices. More than the other major sports, I think, basketball demands the most complete assemblage of talents. A player who has the talent of Jordan surely could be both wide receiver and quarterback (and even, in slightly smaller package, a touch of the defensive end). When we watch them play we are

Patrick Ewing (33) and Scottie Pippen

likely to see the fullest extension of their abilities. When a world-class athlete like Magic Johnson or Julius Erving or Michael Jordan or Scottie Pippen or Shawn Kemp plays in a big game, he plays 35 to 40 minutes of offense and defense. We witness as we rarely do in other sports, the emotions of these athletes. Their emotion is stunningly naked before us.

The timing of Michael Jordan when he arrived in the NBA, destined to be the signature figure not just of that sport but of the professional sports world, could not have been better. He arrived in 1984. There was a sense that he was going to be good, but no one really knew how good, because no one understood his fierce drive to excel. The game was on the rise because of the Magic Johnson/Larry Bird rivalry.

So there was Michael Jordan arriving with his extraordinary body and that dazzling smile (a smile that barely concealed the soul of a samurai warrior underneath). More, even as he arrived, the nature of the American economy was changing, the old blue-collar economy was in decline, the Japanese seemed to do traditional products like automobiles better than we did, and the new world of economic competition for this country was in the world of sneakers and of entertainment; we exported our soft shoes, so to speak, and our entertainment, including sports. Jordan appeared in time to be the centerpiece in an escalating sneaker wars. From the start he got his own line. Nike had come upon stagnant times in the heated sneaker wars and thought it might do around $10 million in business. Instead, the Air Jordan line sold $130 million. Their commercials were brilliantly done, humanizing Jordan as no commercial campaign had ever humanized an athlete before, white or black.

If on the court we saw the ferocity of the warrior, the commercials showed us the charm of the young man inside the warrior. Michael Jordan soon became the most famous athlete, not merely in the country but in the world. His fame and his wealth transcends the game he plays; he is in the broad sense entertainer as well as player. For everything in a media age must entertain — that is his great value, he is not just the ultimate basketball player, he is the ultimate show.

Yet he never confuses his dual roles: compelling athlete and dazzling entertainer. His roots are at least still partially Calvinist; he never confuses what is more important. He rages to be the best, and that fact is obvious to everyone watching him. Where all too many other young men, given that fame and that much money, are content to play at a certain high plateau, Jordan gets better every year, a better defensive player, a smarter, shrewder player, and a better team player. The money from the sneakers and other commercial endorsements, which rep-resents far more than the money he makes from his basketball contract, never distracts

Michael Jordan

him from his real goal, to be the best ever. He never confuses the money, as so many other athletes in all sports do, with being the same as greatness. That is, I suspect, why Michael Jordan is "Michael" to the men who hold the grunt jobs on the street where I live. They know he is obsessed with winning; it is not merely that he wants to win, but that he *has* to win, and they know that although he does not really need the money, he will rise to an ever higher level in big games in order to win. They have seen it in his face. We not only know his moves, after all, but we know his inten-sity. We know he will be up for a big game. We know when he is

disappointed in himself or angry at his teammates, and we know he will push himself, and them, to reach for more. We know when some opposing player has irritated him by mouthing off too soon in a game, and we know Michael is going to pay him back. We know he makes millions, but we do not begrudge him the money, first because we think he has earned it, but perhaps just as much because we have learned something about him over the years, that he does not play for the money, that, like DiMaggio and all those other great athletes before him in this and other sports, he plays to be the best, not just the best today, but the best ever.

And so we have the evolution of these magnificent athletes, from Big Ed Sadowsky to Oscar Robertson, Jerry West and John Havlicek, to, in contemporary setting, Michael. He is the perfect signature player for this astonishing group of NBA athletes in this era. A few years ago I was writing an article about Jordan and I had lunch with Phil Jackson in Seattle. The subject of Michael's moves came up. What thrills the fans, the players and his coaches, Jackson was saying, is that almost every night there is something new and original. It is not, he added, that his hangtime is so great. There may well be people in the league who have greater hangtime. What sets Michael apart, Jackson continued, is what he does in the air, the body control, the vision, the intelligence, the ability to move his body after he has seemingly committed it. If Michael, Jackson notes with a certain delight, is the lineal descen-dant of those great athletes who went before, Elgin Baylor, Connie Hawkins, and Julius Erving, each learning from and expanding upon the accomplishments of the other, then the most exciting question is, what is the next great player going to be able to do?

We give players everything to
help them be successful today.
They have trainers, conditioning coaches,
nutritionists, sports medicine specialists.
**We provide everything except
heart, desire and competitiveness.**
That you can't give a player.

Elgin Baylor

GREEN ROOM

I'm constantly running people off the player floor at their hotels. People now will even check into the team hotel, just so they can see them. We got into one place at 2:30 in the morning, and a five-year-old was waiting with his dad. Five years old! I hear the same things from all the security people at the hotels — they can't believe the people he draws. And these are hotels that are used to dealing with movie stars and politicians. They just can't get over the reaction. And it's everywhere we go.

Sgt. Mike Cofield of the Orange County (Florida) Sheriff's office provided security for Shaquille O'Neal and the Orlando Magic during the 1995-96 season.

One night we're walking toward the Garden to get ready to play against the Knicks, and my guys were with me. We always circled in a group. I looked at the marquee and it says, 'George Mikan vs. The Knicks.' I thought, 'Oh boy, they shouldn't have done that.' So we get into the locker room and they were really giving it to me. As you notice, I wore glasses, so I took them off so I could get into my uniform. I got ready to go out and play, put my glasses back on and no one else had changed. They looked at me and said, 'OK, big shot. If you're going out to play them, then go ahead. It says you against the Knicks.' They really razzed me for quite a while. The following day they had me go up on the ladder. But I used my head a little bit. I gave a copy of the picture to each one of my teammates. 'OK, now you won't forget it.' Really, it was both thrilling and embarrassing to see your name on the Madison Square Garden marquee.

As the league's first superstar, George Mikan was sometimes sent into a city a day early to hype the next night's game.
Not only would Mikan go to various radio stations for interviews, but in towns such as Boston and New York,
he would meet individually with dozens of sportswriters.

Michael Jordan is the greatest practice player in the history of sports.

Jerry Krause, Chicago's vice president of operations, was one of the NBA's first full-time scouts in the early 1960s prior to building the Bulls' four championship teams in the 1990s.

I have always approached practice as a kind of proving ground. That's especially true with rookies. They might have seen me on television, read about me in newspapers and they might think they know what I'm all about or what it's like to play against me. So I feel like I have a reputation to defend. And I am going to defend that reputation. I want them to know what they might have heard isn't gossip or rumors. I want them to know it all comes from hard work. When they come into the Chicago Bulls' camp, they're going to see everything I have and I'm going to find out whether they can compete with me. It's no different with a veteran that joins our team. If I'm considered one of the best players in the game, then I want to show them there's a reason for that. And the reason is that I practice harder and I do all the necessary things to get to that level. I want them to know I deserve what I get. I want them to know the whole experience is real. And it all starts in practice.

Michael Jordan played in 659 of the 666 games in which he was eligible to appear from the start of the 1986-87 season through 1995-96.

I didn't want to play for the Celtics because they won a championship and all their players were returning. But Red Auerbach cut a guy who wasn't in shape. I came to camp in shape so I made the team. That's how it was in those days.

Sam Jones, a Hall of Fame shooting guard and the eighth player chosen in the 1957 NBA Draft, played on 10 Boston championship teams during his 12 seasons with the Celtics through 1968-69.

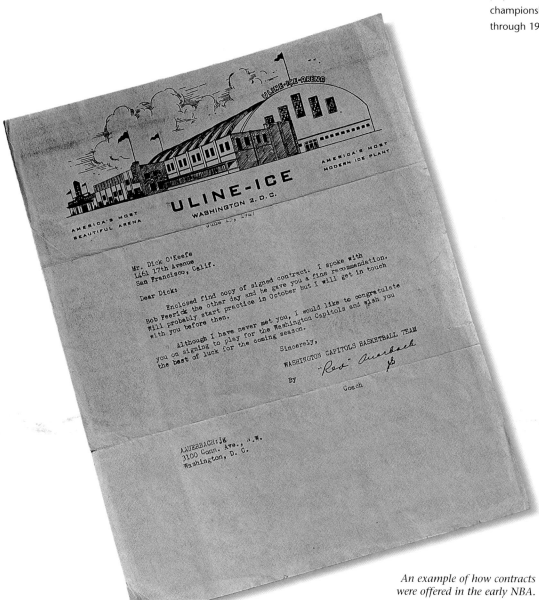

An example of how contracts were offered in the early NBA.

Red called me up and asked me if I wanted to play for the Celtics. I was out of college and playing baseball and I wasn't really interested in going east. Red said, 'Well, you can make some good money if you make the team. If you make the team, I'll pay your way back home. If you don't make the team, then you'll have to pay.' It was 1952 and I was 21 years old. I went

upstairs to see Mr. Walter Brown and Red Auerbach after I worked out and Red says, 'I think we can keep you. We better discuss salary.' I asked him what he paid his people. And Red says, 'Walter Brown paid the entire team $87,000 last season.' I'm thinking they have Bill Sharman, Ed Macauley, Bob Cousy. What should I ask for? I'm trying to figure it out in my head, and

said, 'How about $5,000?' He looked at me kind of funny, so I said, 'How about $4,500?' Red said it sounds good. That's how I became a Celtic.

Gene Conley was a Major League Baseball pitcher in and around six seasons with the Boston Celtics from 1952 through 1960-61.

It isn't an in-your-face kind of challenge. It's developing a philosophy whereby that team

knows what they're doing has a chance to create some significance in their lives.

They can be part of a championship team. They can be part of a team that's growing and

developing. And the only way you're ever going to grow, really grow,

is each and every day you've got to come in and look each other in the eye.

And you have to look after one another.

I do challenge the players.

I do confront them.

I do have great demands on them for their time and for their energy and for their spirit.

And I think that's important in order to get the best out of these players.

Pat Riley played on the Lakers' 1972 title team and later coached the Los Angeles Lakers
to seven Finals appearances and four NBA championships in nine years. No coach has won more playoff games.

A lot of times a silent moment is sometimes how we start out. Let's take a few deep breaths, be quiet and settle in. Be quiet until we can still ourselves a little bit and listen. Stop the inner motors from working in the mind.

Phil Jackson won an NBA title as a player with the New York Knicks and four as coach of the Chicago Bulls. Through the 1995-96 season, no coach with 200 or more NBA wins had a higher winning percentage (.721) than Jackson.

I was really a novelty when I became a player-coach because only Bill Russell had done it previously. The biggest problem I felt was that guys I had played with all of a sudden wanted to take advantage of me. I had to really make an effort to get on them to be in shape and work hard. I didn't have any problems substituting for myself, though, because I understood the game and I knew that if I wasn't doing the job I needed to be out of there so I wouldn't hurt the team.

I don't think you could do it today — not unless you had a couple of assistants who you really felt good about and let them run the show for you. There's too much to watch, too much to teach, egos are too big. I don't think you could do it effectively today.

Lenny Wilkens started his coaching career in 1969 while he was still an All-Star point guard for the Seattle SuperSonics, whom he later led to the 1979 NBA title.

Head coach Lenny Wilkens talks to the 1996 USA Basketball team.

We wanted to treat Bill Russell

the same way we treated Red,

but Russell was also a player. We had to figure out,

how do we talk to Russell in a ballgame?

Do we talk to him as a player

or do we approach him as a coach?

We respected him but we did not go out with him.

All of the sudden he became the lonely man

because we didn't socialize with him anymore like

we did before he became coach.

Celtics guard Sam Jones.

Bill Russell

Larry Bird came to practice every day focused. There was no goofing around once he was on the floor. It was serious business. The first couple years we tried to beat him to practice. Or we'd try to be the last ones to leave.

But he was the first one there and the last one to leave.

We'd stick around and shoot or play these little games. And we'd look down to the other end and think, 'Yeah, he's still there.' We'd stay a little longer, two hours after practice. Larry would still be down there shooting. You'd think, 'Well, he beat me today. I've got things to do. I've got a life!' So when it came time for the game, you knew he was ready because you had watched him do all those things every day in practice to get himself ready.

M.L. Carr played on two Boston championship teams with Larry Bird before moving into the Celtics' front office and taking over as head coach of the team in 1995.

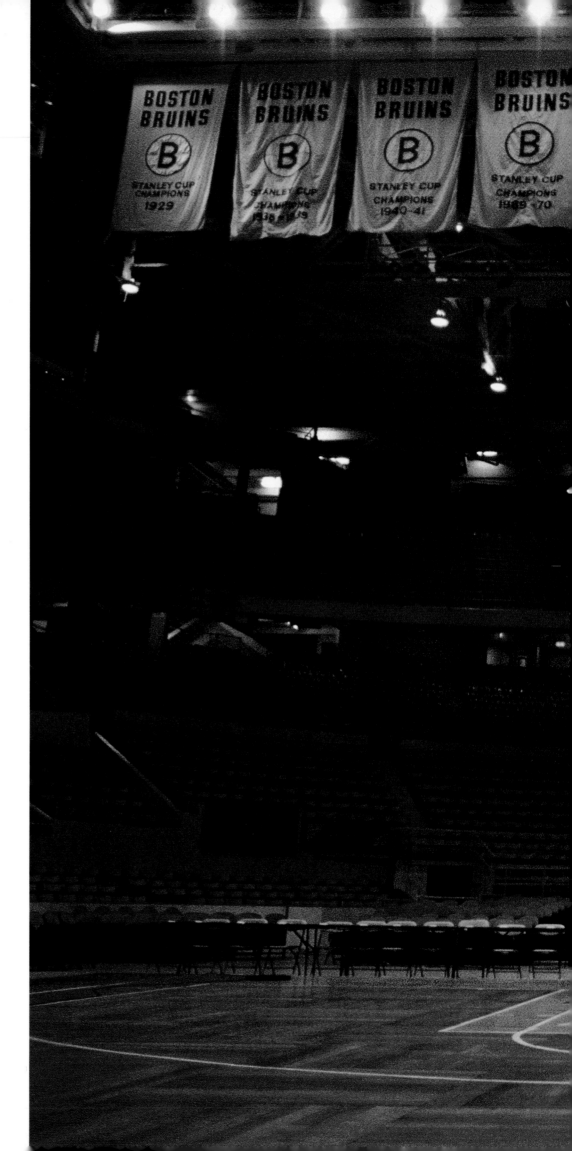

Larry Bird

People probably envisioned yoga as too esoteric. They didn't envision themselves

sitting in a room staring at a spot on the wall. My yoga isn't like that. It's really intense

Kareem Abdul-Jabbar played an NBA record 57,446 minutes during his 20-year career. Robert Parish, the only other player to play as many as 20 years, finished the 1995-96 season more than 12,000 minutes, or 250 complete games behind Abdul-Jabbar.

stretching and it works the whole body through the whole range of motion. I wouldn't

have played as long if it wasn't for my yoga class. I would have been too stiff or some-

thing would have happened. The stretching maximizes physical potential because you can count on not getting hurt because muscle pulls and tears don't occur. So your

endurance and strength are maximized by your body's ability not to get tied up. The

Abdul-Jabbar scored 38,387 points, nearly 7,000 more than Wilt Chamberlain and nearly 14,000 more than Michael Jordan through the 1995-96 season.

In 1985, at the age of 38, he was named Most Valuable Player of the NBA Finals. A year later, Abdul-Jabbar was named to All-NBA First Team.

meditation part of the type of yoga I do is included in what I'm doing physically. A lot

of the positions involve standing on one leg so you have to concentrate on the balance

point. There aren't two of them so you have to really stay on one point.

Kareem Abdul-Jabbar played 1,560 games, or an average of 78 games per season, during his 20 NBA seasons from 1969 through 1988-89.

I had a broken nose, broken hands, stress fractures in my feet. You just went out and played. You were expected to play. You got to the point where later on in your years, you'd lie there on the training table and you'd rub your leg and you'd say, **'C'mon leg, c'mon. Just give me one more game. I'll quit after this. Just one more game. That's all I want.'** You'd go out and play that one game, then the next game you'd be there on the training table and you'd say, 'You know I like to lie a little bit, legs. You know that. But this time, I'm serious. Give me one more game.' And the legs would give you one more game.

Johnny "Red" Kerr was the NBA's first Iron Man, playing in 844 consecutive games
between 1954 and 1965, the second longest streak in history behind Randy Smith's 906.

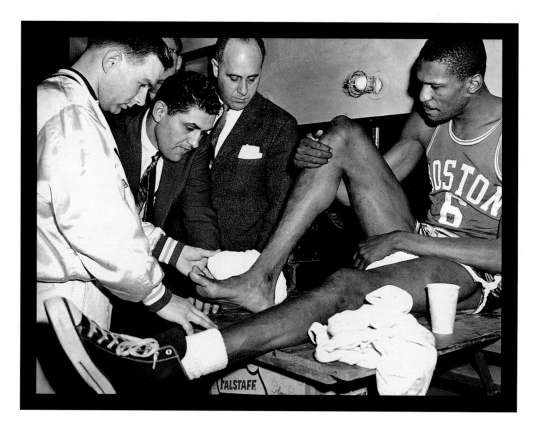

Boston Celtics great, Bill Russell, has his right foot examined
as coach Red Auerbach (third from left) looks on.

My body was not meant to play the way I do. I'm shorter than most of the guys who play up front in the NBA, the guys who play elbow wars every night, so I've always known that some day it would take its toll, that my body would just give in to the pounding it took 82 nights during the regular season and playoffs. But that was okay. It was a sacrifice I had decided to make. I always knew I only had a certain amount of time in this game and that the bumps, bruises, strains and sprains could heal up when I was through.

Charles Barkley, just 6-feet-6, won the 1986-87 rebound title by averaging 14.6 a game;
the rest of the top five that season had an average height of nearly 6-feet-11.

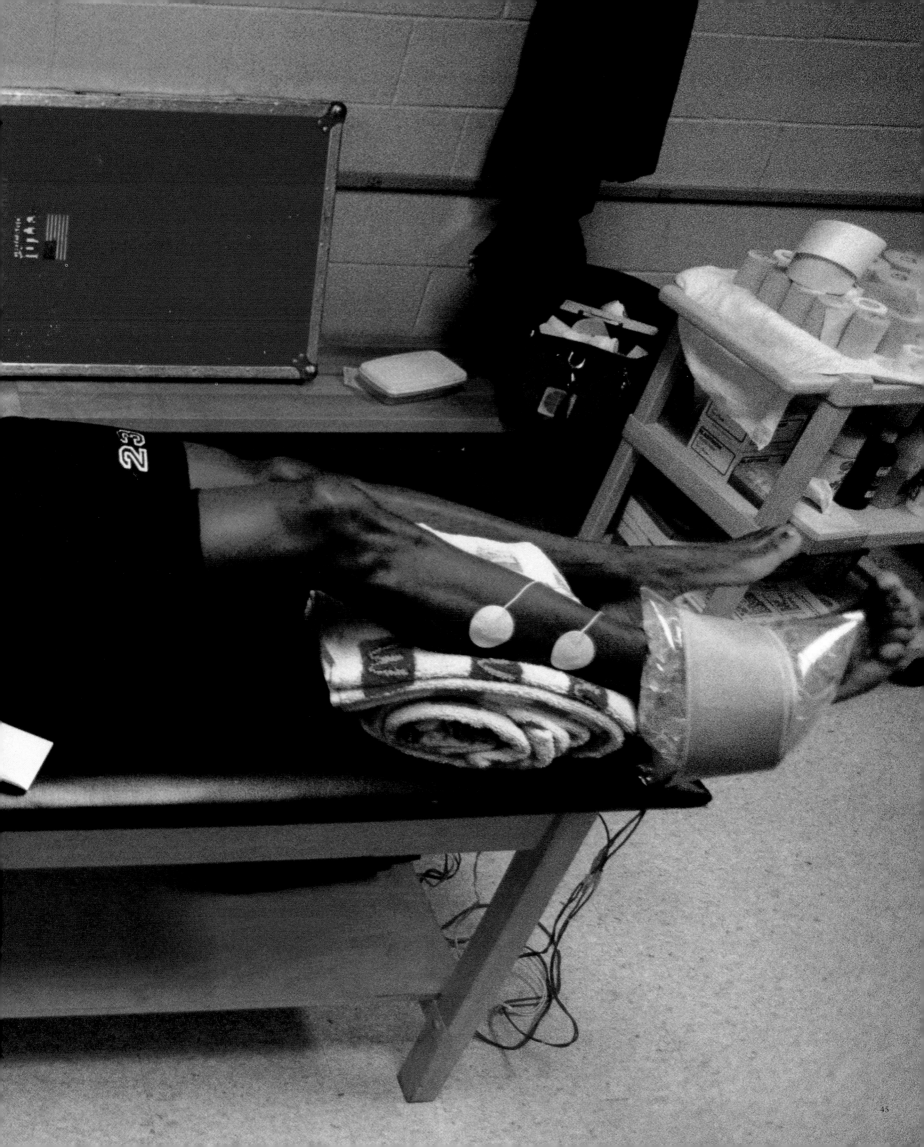

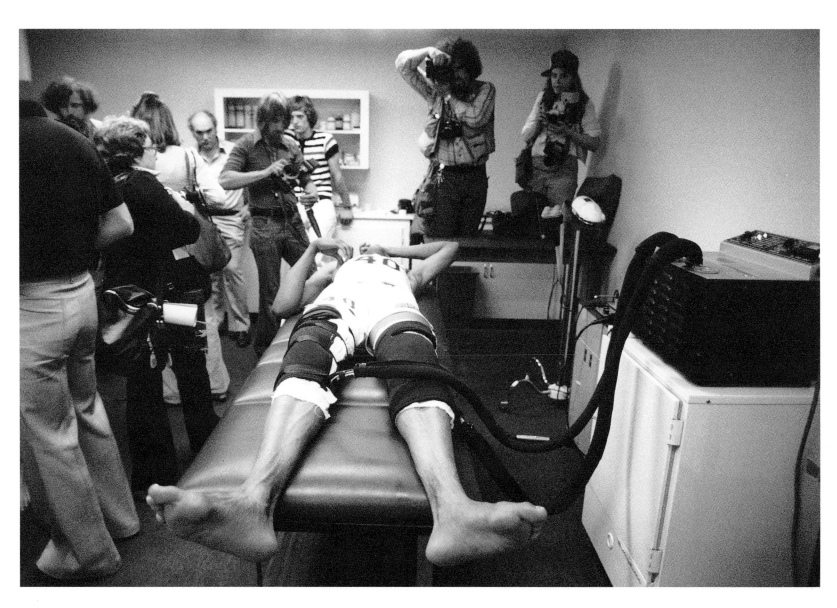

Seattle SuperSonics center Marvin Webster has cold packs, an innovative procedure at the time, applied to his aching knees during the 1978 Finals against the Washington Bullets.

Boston's Satch Sanders (16) and Larry Siegfried.

From 1963 until I retired in 1971, I had tendinitis and calcium deposits lodged around the tendons in both knees. Then, in the first game of the 1965 playoffs, I split my kneecap and tore the patella tendon. The doctor walked in and said, 'I don't think you'll be able to play basketball again.' So I asked him if I'd be able to walk normal. He said, 'You might, but as far as your basketball career, that's it.' At that time this was considered a career-ending injury. But it happened in April and in September I came back and played. I probably shouldn't have because it was never right.

My knees were so bad I couldn't even drive to games. Either someone had to drive me or I had to catch a cab because my knees were so stiff. One reason is because I'd cover them in heat packs which I know now is about the dumbest thing to do. **No one knew about ice then.** After games I'd get in a nice hot tub just to relieve some of the ache.

Julius Erving cools his jets.

But a little while after I got out, the inflammation was so bad I couldn't move. And we didn't have fluid removed from knees like they do today. **So I'd have cortisone injections about three times a week.** It got to the point the injections didn't even work. So I'd be eight or nine minutes into the game before my knees got loose to the point I could play.

Elgin Baylor averaged 23.6 points, 11.1 rebounds and 38 minutes a game in the five years following his career-threatening knee injury.

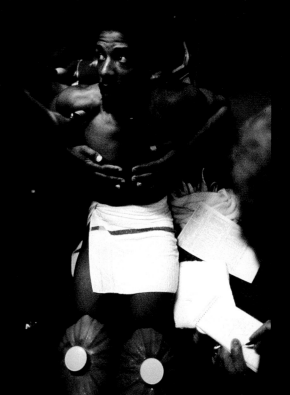

Just in the six years between coaching Chicago and coming back with Detroit, the difference is amazing. You have your own practice facility, your own plane, your own strength and conditioning coach, your own physical therapist, your own nutritionist. Guys who aren't married hire cooks to come in so they make sure they're eating properly. We didn't understand training. My body broke down because I overtrained. I was so driven I broke my body down. Now, I look at our locker room before the game and one guy's getting a massage, another is being stretched by our conditioning guy. We never had that. Even the footwear. We wore shoes that had no arches. It was like running on cement. And the travel. When we play in Chicago now, after the game we get on the plane with food waiting. Our guys are home in their own beds by 1:30 in the morning. When I played, we'd have a five o'clock wake-up call, get on a bus, get to the airport, sit in the terminal, grab the plane, travel the day of the game. The difference in training and nutrition and everything that goes with it is incredible. Look at a guy like Scottie Pippen compared to when he came into the league.

It's enabled guys to get stronger, stay healthier and play longer.

The players are our assets and ownership realized they had to have these things available to protect those assets.

Detroit Pistons head coach Doug Collins was a four-time All-Star during his eight NBA seasons between 1973 and 1981, despite averaging just 52 games a year due to injuries.

Scottie Pippen

49

I dressed in black before games because
I felt black was kind of sinister.
It kind of let everyone know I meant business.
Before Game 6 in 1971, the year Baltimore
finally beat the Knicks,
I went out and bought an all-black outfit.
The only thing that wasn't black
was the red hatband on my hat.
They asked me why I dressed like that.
I said, 'Because I mean business tonight.'

Earl "The Pearl" Monroe scored 27 points and had 7 assists in Game 6 of the 1971 Eastern Conference Finals.

GAME FACE

renas were available certain nights of the week. And in Rochester, the Edgerton Park Arena was available on Saturday nights. Fort Wayne was available on Sundays and very often teams would have to travel from Rochester after a Saturday night game to Fort Wayne. But there's no way to get there, really. So a method was devised. I was broadcasting the Knicks games at the time and we would race from the game to the train station before midnight to catch the 20th Century Limited going through Chicago. Then, at five in the morning, the porter would come through and wake everyone and the train would make a non-scheduled stop in the middle of a prairie in Indiana. With dawn just breaking we'd climb down onto a platform. There was no overhead to this platform, just a platform in the middle of a prairie. The train would take off immediately. So the ten ball players, coach Joe Lapchick

and I would get down off this platform and there we were. But our instructions were to look in the distance and see a blinking amber light on a crossroad, oh, about a half mile in the distance. So we'd take a walk down this blacktop road and come to this crossroad where the light was blinking. It was a small community, the tallest house being perhaps two, two and a half stories high. Our instructions were to go around the corner to the Green Parrot Cafe. Now the Green Parrot Cafe was a bar with a green parrot on it. And it was dark with just this blinking amber light. And our instructions further told us to take a pebble and throw it up to the second-floor window a couple times. And Carl Braun used to do this because he had a nice soft touch. He'd throw it up to the second floor, wake up the manager and we went right up to bed. Then we'd play that afternoon or evening.

Marty Glickman, a sprinter on the 1936 Men's Olympic team, broadcast New York Knicks games for 11 years between 1946 and 1964.

The 1995-96 Orlando Magic team jet.

Traveling by train in those days was not the easiest thing to do. And, I hate to say it, but most players would have two or three beers before they would try to hit that sleeping compartment. Now you had guys that were 6-feet-6, 6-feet-7, 6-feet-8, trying to sleep all doubled up in a 6-foot compartment. So you would hope that you could have a couple beers and get drowsy enough to sleep. It was very tough, particularly for guys my size. Today they have these Hollywood-type beds that have no footboard. You go in, lie down and it's fine if you have your feet hanging over the end. When we played, the beds had these big footboards. You had to take the dresser drawers out, pile them up and put pillows on top to extend the bed. They didn't have televisions in the room that worked. They had radios, but you had to put in a quarter to get an hour's worth of radio. There would be guys putting hangers and things in there, turning them around just so they could get the radio to work for two or three hours without using another quarter.

Johnny "Red" Kerr, 6-feet-9 and 230 pounds, didn't miss a game during his first 11 NBA seasons.

Bill Sharman, Bill Russell and Bob Cousy check into a hotel on the road.

Michael Jordan in his suite at The Plaza in New York.

Michael Jordan

Ervin Johnson

Hersey Hawkins

Nate McMillan

Scottie Pippen

Shawn Kemp

Dennis Rodman

Gary Payton

Toni Kukoc

Frank Brickowski

Ron Harper

Detlef Schremp

I have heard players that played in Boston Garden say the visiting locker room was overheated and all kinds of other stuff. In fact, we were treated as poorly as the visitors by Boston Garden management in my early days with the Celtics. Our locker room, in the heyday when we were winning all those championships, consisted of

two nails for everybody.

I was stationed between Bill Russell and Bob Cousy, practically in the corner. We had one shower that would overflow and flood the locker room so everybody would rush to get out fast so their shoes wouldn't get wet. In Philadelphia, you'd go play at Convention Hall and you didn't even get a hook. We used to lay our clothes out on a table in some dingy conference room. So facilities weren't the best. Nowadays players go first class, everybody has their own room. Never happened in my day.

Tom Heinsohn played on eight Boston championship teams before leading the Celtics to two more titles as their head coach in 1974 and 1976.

Visiting locker room at the the United Center in Chicago prior to Game 1 of the 1996 NBA Finals between the Bulls and Seattle SuperSonics.

I wanted players to play hard, play together and to play the team game. I also wanted to help them by constructing an approach that would utilize their talents best. I wanted them to feel on top of the game strategically so they knew I was going to help them win by the tactics or substitutions I made, by the preparation before the game. It is a unique experience. Coaching requires so many qualities. It's like conducting an orchestra, getting all the parts to play in harmony so that what comes out of all these instruments is a pleasing sound, a positive, beautiful sound.

Jack Ramsay coached four NBA teams to 864 victories in 21 seasons, the fifth highest total behind Lenny Wilkens, Red Auerbach, Dick Motta and Bill Fitch.

Pat Riley, then head coach of the New York Knicks, finds solitude in the visiting shower area prior to Game 7 of the 1994 NBA Finals in Houston.

Orlando assistant coach Richie Adubato.

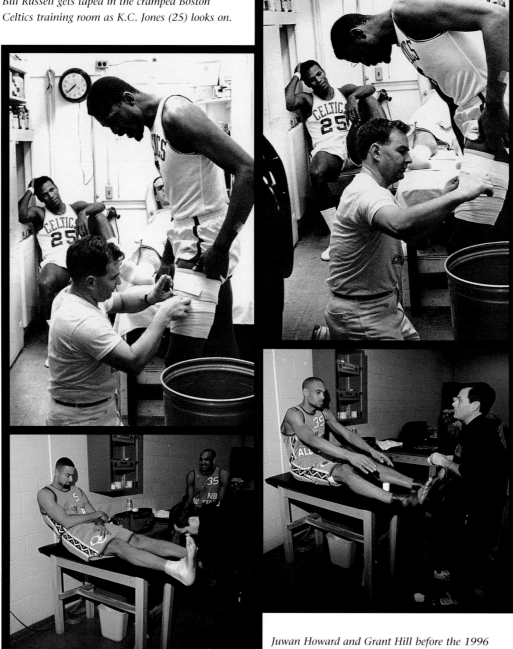

Bill Russell gets taped in the cramped Boston Celtics training room as K.C. Jones (25) looks on.

Juwan Howard and Grant Hill before the 1996 All-Star Game.

When I first came into the league, many times we didn't have a trainer around. I taped my own ankles for 11 years. And you played whether you were hurt or not. I remember spraining my ankle one night so badly I couldn't get up out of bed the next morning. Two teammates carried me down to the elevator, put me in a cab and carried me onto the train. I played that night. You just taped it up and went at it. I also broke my arm one night and I played the next night. I only played for a minute or two, but in those days you played. If you were hurt, you better really be hurt. I mean a broken bone or something like that. In my case, that didn't keep me out but a day or two. There was pressure on you to play, particularly if you were an integral part of the team.

Bob Pettit missed only nine games from the start of the 1954-55 season through 1963-64.

Michael Jordan

Walt Frazier

I can remember as a young player a scouting report was something like, 'Well, you know you're going to play Oscar tonight. He's going to back you down, so try to be physical with him.' And that was it! Today it's much more intricate. We look at video, we break things down for individual players. We know the other team's strengths, weaknesses, all that kind of stuff.

Lenny Wilkens was an All-Star point guard nine times during his 15 NBA seasons from 1961 through 1974-75.

We were in the playoffs one year and
I had made the pregame talk very quick,
very easy and very relaxed. They went out
there to warm up and I always went out with
them and watched. I was standing there and

I thought, 'Gee, Russell forgot to vomit.'

Because he always vomited before a big game.
So, I thought I'd try something. I called the
team off the court and I sent them all back
into the locker room. And I was a pacer.
I paced back and forth for five or six seconds.
I turned around and glared at Russell.
I said, 'Russell, go vomit.' All the players were
sitting there and they couldn't understand
why I had taken them off the court. I didn't
want to take Russell off by himself, that
was ridiculous. People would say,
'What's wrong with him?' So he went and
vomited and we went out and won the game,
you see. It worked.

Red Auerbach coached the Boston Celtics from
1950 through the 1965-66 season.

*Denver guard Mark Jackson's pregame ritual includes
tying his wedding ring to his left shoe.*

I didn't even know who was in the stands when I played. I looked down when I ran onto the court and I looked down when I ran off. I never made any eye contact, period. I had a ritual. I did the same thing every day of my life for 14 years. I got up in the morning and had breakfast. What I ate varied as people talked about the different things you should eat. But I used to eat my pregame meal four hours before the game. After the game I'd rarely eat anything more than a half of a sandwich, something like that. I would take a nap every afternoon and I'd be the first one to the game. I would be the last one to dress. The locker room was my sanctuary. I did these things religiously for 14 years. It was a discipline I felt I had to maintain to play the game correctly and not cheat the fans. I understood that I had been given a gift to play the game.

Jerry West was elected to the Naismith Memorial Basketball Hall of Fame in 1979.

When I came into the league, the developmental program for referees consisted of meeting with Mendy (Rudolph) for dinner and talking about what was going on in the game. We had no film or videotape. We were sitting in Downey's Restaurant in New York with Mendy drawing on napkins. Now we might watch three or four hours a day of tape with the young referees.

Videotape has created a dramatic change. We tape the games out of the television feed into our locker room. We look at tape at halftime. I might have a play at 2:32 of the second quarter, make a mental note of it, and go in at halftime and run the tape back to that point. Sometimes, we go out on the floor at halftime and tell the player what we saw on the tape.

I was teaching school and coaching high school football outside of Philadelphia in 1966. I had no intention of making this my profession. I was enjoying life and had some goals, one of which was to be Joe Paterno. The referee job had no benefits and it paid $75 a game. But I was single and I could see the country. That was all I intended to do.

Ed T. Rush (middle) started his career as an NBA referee in 1966, and through 1995-96 had officiated league games for 30 seasons.

I had worked in the league for two or three years and in those days I had started out in 1953 making $40.00 a game. And every year you got a $5 raise. Mr. Podoloff, who was the commissioner then, would give you an automatic raise if you were retained. So, after working for two to three years I thought I was worth more than a $5 raise. And I called the league office. In those days there were only three people in the league office. It was Mr. Podoloff, Haskell Cohen, the public relations director and Connie Meriselli, who was the assistant to the commissioner. And I arranged to come up and visit the commissioner. Mr. Podoloff, who was about 5-feet-5, sat behind a large desk in the Empire State Building. When I came up he greeted me by saying, 'Mr. Referee, what can I do for you?' I knew I was in trouble when he didn't even know my name. But I explained to him that I worked in the league several years and because of my good work I thought I was entitled to a $10 raise. You can see that I was a great negotiator. And with that, he stood up to his full height of 5-feet-5, or whatever he was, he slammed his fist upon the table and he said, 'Are you trying to bankrupt the NBA?' To this day, I don't know if I hadn't taken a $5 raise whether the NBA would have been successful. So, I tell people I saved the NBA from bankruptcy.

Norm Drucker worked 14 years as an NBA official from 1953 through 1967 and learned to avoid getting pelted with debris by fans by "standing near the home team's huddle during timeouts."

The late Earl Strom was an NBA referee for 33 seasons from 1957 through 1989-90.

It's the industry the city promotes. It's Hollywood. It's Showtime. (Owner) Dr. Buss believed in it and he wanted a different style of atmosphere. He wanted the Laker Girls. He wanted the actors and actresses sitting in his seats and it

all transferred right onto the floor. He wanted a fast-paced, exciting ball game and it promoted the industry this city already had in place. Showtime was definitely geared toward us.

James Worthy was the No. 1 pick in the 1982 NBA Draft by Los Angeles, the result of a trade engineered by general manager Jerry West, who dealt Don Ford and a first-round draft pick to Cleveland for the rights to the Cavaliers' 1982 first-round pick.

Dec. 22, 1949, that was the night I made my accordion debut for the Boston Celtics. That night the Celtics, for the first time in their four years of existence, whipped the Lakers. And fabulous Tony Lavelli hit for 26 points, plus getting a rave review on the accordion. I hit for six points in the first half, then about 20 in the second after doing the halftime show. The halftime shows today, with the Laker Girls and such, are fabulous. It's entertainment that goes back to the Roman circuses. And I've performed with some of the greatest circus acts in the world.

Tony Lavelli played a total of 86 games for Boston and New York from 1949-1951 and along the way sometimes provided the halftime entertainment by playing his accordion.

Once it's time to take care of business, all that other stuff you put on the side.

You and I might be friends off the court, but on the court you better do what

we need to get done out there or we're going to be adversaries.

Isiah Thomas led the Detroit Pistons to the NBA Finals three straight years (1988-90). After losing to the Lakers and good friend Magic Johnson in 1989, Thomas and the Pistons came back to win the title on the Lakers' home court in 1990.

Kareem Abdul-Jabbar ◦ Nate Archibald ◦ Paul Arizin ◦ Charles Barkley
Rick Barry ◦ Elgin Baylor ◦ Dave Bing ◦ Larry Bird ◦ Wilt Chamberlain
Bob Cousy ◦ Dave Cowens ◦ Billy Cunningham ◦ Dave DeBusschere
Clyde Drexler ◦ Julius Erving ◦ Patrick Ewing ◦ Walt Frazier
George Gervin ◦ Hal Greer ◦ John Havlicek ◦ Elvin Hayes
Earvin Johnson ◦ Sam Jones ◦ Michael Jordan ◦ Jerry Lucas

The NBA extended invitations to a panel of 50 experts and asked them to vote on the 50 greatest players in NBA history. Each panel member voted for 50 players in no particular order, and the 50 who received the most votes are featured in *The NBA at 50*. The panel represented a wide spectrum of experts, each of whom had a unique view of NBA history. Included were team executives and coaches, veteran members of print and electronic media and some of the greatest players in NBA history.

Karl Malone ◦ Moses Malone ◦ Pete Maravich ◦ Kevin McHale
George Mikan ◦ Earl Monroe ◦ Shaquille O'Neal ◦ Hakeem Olajuwon
Robert Parish ◦ Bob Pettit ◦ Scottie Pippen ◦ Willis Reed
Oscar Robertson ◦ David Robinson ◦ Bill Russell ◦ Dolph Schayes
Bill Sharman ◦ John Stockton ◦ Isiah Thomas ◦ Nate Thurmond
Wes Unseld ◦ Bill Walton ◦ Jerry West ◦ Lenny Wilkens ◦ James Worthy

FIFTY PLAYERS

11 rings

Winning is the only thing
I really cared about because
I found that when I left
the cocoon of my childhood
I came into the world
and found that individual awards
were mostly political.
But winning and losing,
there are no politics,
only numbers.

It's the most democratic thing
in the world. You either win or lose.
So I decided early in my career
that the only really important thing
was to try and win every game
because when I got through
no one could say,
'Well, he was the best at this or that.'
The only thing that
really mattered was who won.

And there is nothing subjective about that.

Bill Russell led the University of San Francisco to two NCAA championships,
the U.S. Men's basketball team to the Gold Medal in the 1956 Olympics and
the Boston Celtics to 11 championships in 13 seasons between
1956 and 1969, the last three as player-coach.

COOZ

Cousy was the best playmaking guard that ever played the game. That's why our offense worked so well. We only had six plays and everybody was a double-digit scorer. He would pick the hot hand and knew where the weakness was in the other team's defensive alignment. I don't think there's ever been another that's matched him. He wasn't very fast, but he was the best passer, bar none, including the great Magic Johnson, who everybody considers innovative. Have you ever seen a guy throw a hook pass the length of the court off a made free throw to a guy to score on a fast break? I don't think you have.

Tom Heinsohn was on the receiving end of Bob Cousy passes on six Boston championship teams from 1957 through 1963.

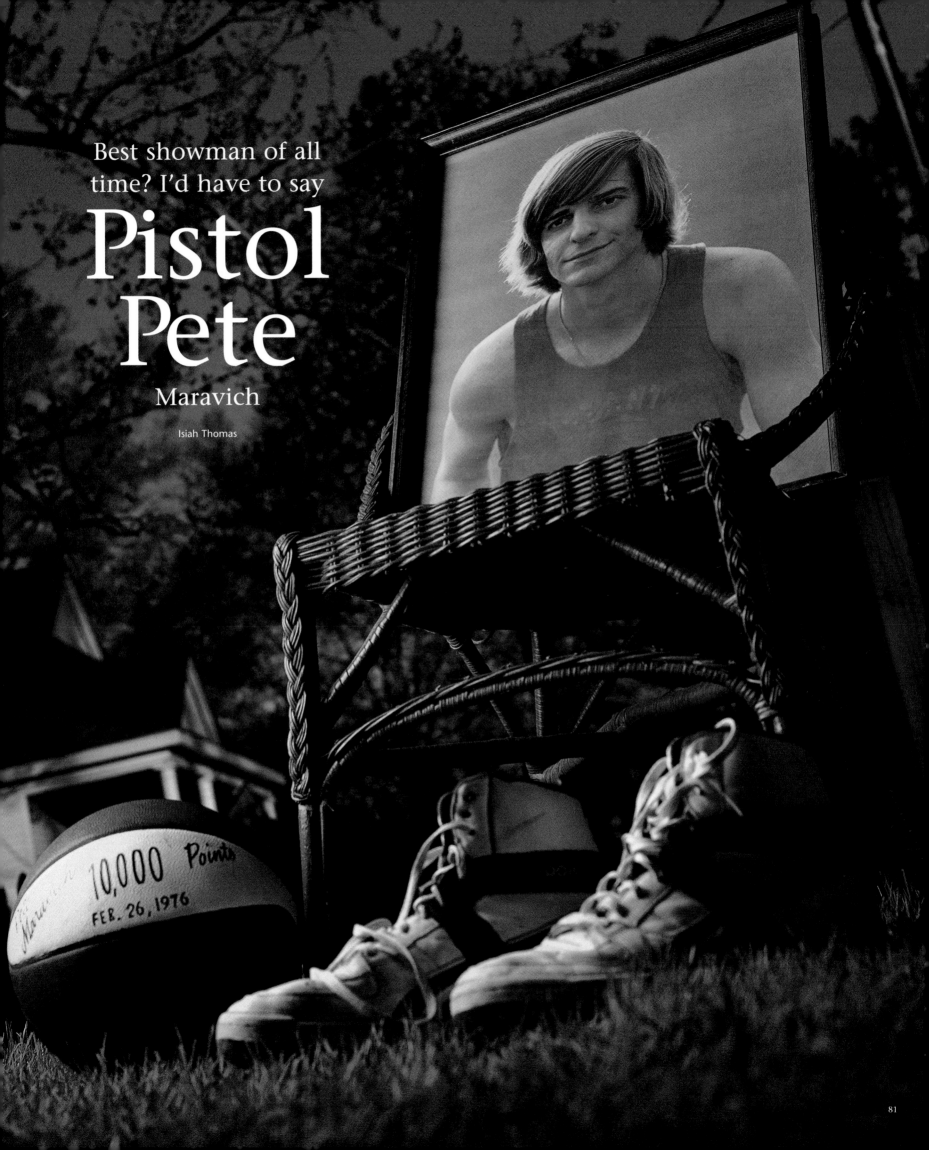

Best showman of all time? I'd have to say

Pistol Pete

Maravich

Isiah Thomas

10,000 Points
FEB. 26, 1976

81

Walt Frazier

was the epitome of cool, not only the way he dressed but the way he played the game. I mean, do you remember Walter Frazier ever really sweating?

Steve "Snapper" Jones

Sam Jones showed up at the most crucial times to get the good shot.

He was a great shooter, a great defensive player and he had great speed. There wasn't anything Sam Jones couldn't do. If he had played with a team other than the Celtics, he'd be held in the same esteem as Jerry West or Oscar Robertson. He was the guy that wanted to take the crucial shot. And if he asked for it, you knew he could deliver.

John Havlicek on Sam Jones. Havlicek and Jones played on six Boston championship teams from 1963 through 1969.

Zen Archery involves that quiet intensity. People have been sent to study Zen Archery just so they can learn to concen-

trate because there's a whole system of getting physically ready, having your equipment ready, knowing your target and

becoming part of the target. By sending the arrow into the target you are really sending the arrow back toward yourself.

That's the thought process involved. I was fortunate to be into those types of things at an early point in my life and I tried

to incorporate them into my basketball game.

Kareem Abdul-Jabbar attempted a record 15,837 field goals and connected on 55.9 percent of them during his 20 NBA seasons.

Isiah

Isiah Thomas was the very best at what he did. He was a point guard that could score 20 to 25 points a game and he could control the tempo. On the fast break he's always going to hit the open man and make the right play. Down the stretch he's going to find a way to beat you. I don't care if he makes the last-second shot or he sets up one of his teammates. He's going to find a way to beat the opposing team.

Sidney Moncrief was a four-time member of the NBA All-Defense First Team and played against Thomas between 1981 and 1991.

Billy Cunningham had tremendous jumping ability, was an extraordinarily good passer and as fierce a competitor as you will ever find. A lot of people referred to him as "The Kangaroo Kid" because of his great leaping ability. But it was his body control and his competitiveness that put him at another level. A lot of guys can jump, but they can't do things up in the air like he did. Special players can go up, turn their body, take some contact and score. Billy was great at finishing off plays.

Rod Thorn has been a player, coach, team executive and league executive
since the Baltimore Bullets made him a first-round draft pick in 1963.

THE CAPTAIN

Knicks fans have a proprietary interest in Willis Reed. He is always their captain, a heroic figure in the classical sense. New Yorkers somehow learn that it was Willis, wounded as he was, who came off the trainer's table to win the championship in 1970. When Joe DiMaggio walks down the street, when Jack Dempsey walks into a restaurant, they're still New Yorkers. Willis approaches that.   Michael Burke, former president of the New York Knicks.

One of the things I learned early in my career,
even in college, was how to play to the crowd.
And it became very important to me to have the crowd on
my side because it just made my juices flow.
The things I did on the court, a lot of times were instinctive.
But at the same time, I knew exactly what we were doing.

Earl "The Pearl" Monroe played nine seasons with the New York Knicks
from 1971 through 1980-81 and is considered one of the most dazzling
ballhandlers and scorers in NBA history.

Earl the Pearl

Enthusiasm is something that comes from inside. And Earvin Johnson embodied this in a natural state. It wasn't something he had to fabricate or manufacture. He had a passion, simply a passion, an incredible passion to play basketball. He was playing a game that men were being paid to play and treated it like it was a kid's game. But he also wanted to win. He wore this passion, this enthusiasm on his sleeve. He let everyone know how happy he was to be playing this game. Somewhere along the way he found an incredible desire to want to play basketball. And I think that passion manifested itself in one of the great personalities in the history of professional basketball. People gravitate toward Earvin. Anyone that could have that much fun on the court, even though at times he was going through tremendous pain because of the pressure of trying to produce and perform, understands exactly what greatness is all about. It's about passion. And there isn't anybody who showed that kind of passion more than Earvin.

Pat Riley coached Earvin "Magic" Johnson's Los Angeles Lakers to four NBA championships between 1981 and 1988.

SCOTTIE PIPPEN HAS GOT TO BE CONSIDERED ONE OF THE BEST ALL-AROUND PLAYERS IN THE GAME. WHEN ONE PHASE OF HIS GAME IS NOT ON KEY, HE'S ABLE TO CONTRIBUTE IN OTHER WAYS. I THINK THAT'S THE SIGN OF GREATNESS.

Michael Jordan on Scottie Pippen. They are the only teammates to be named to the All-NBA First Team and the All-Defensive First Team in the same season.

I believed the game in the post was about physics. If I could beat you to point B, then I might be able to beat you to point C. So I had my areas where I knew I could get to and what moves I was going to make when I got there. If you defended me three or four different ways, then I had three or four different moves. It was something I worked at, but I always believed I was quicker than most forwards I played against.

BIG GAME JAMES

A

B

C

James Worthy earned his nickname, Big Game James, for a series of brilliant playoff performances in crucial games, including a triple double — 36 points, 16 rebounds and 10 assists — against Detroit in Game 7 of the 1988 NBA Finals that secured the Los Angeles Lakers' fifth championship in nine years.

Am I the greatest?

I think I could have played against anybody and played very well against anybody. No one's going to ever know who's the greatest

basketball player. I think I'm the greatest — look at my record. They look at a guy who dunks the ball today, they think that's great.

Oscar Robertson averaged

a triple double —

You dunk the ball and can't make a free throw? Can't make a play? You can't set up an offense? You don't know when to slow the ball

30.8 points,

12.5 rebounds,

11.4 assists —

down or when to speed it up? You don't know who's hot? You don't know who can't guard from the other side? You don't know the

during the 1961-62 season.

No other player has ever come close.

intangible things about basketball? I played as well as I could. I tried to conduct myself the way I was taught by my coaches, my

parents. That's all you can give and let the cards fall where they may.

When you talk about the greatest players ever, Hakeem Olajuwon's got to be very high on the list. Look at all the things he can do. Who else that size can play the game like he does? He's got the body of a center, but the moves of a small forward. There are some guards who can't move like he does. And he makes all his teammates better, at both ends of the court. He's a happy, honest, humble guy, and that's rare for somebody with his ability.

Clyde Drexler on Hakeem Olajuwon, a two-time Finals MVP.
Drexler and Olajuwon helped the Houston Rockets to the 1995 NBA Championship.

Hakeem

The thing I like most about
Patrick Ewing
is his mental toughness.
He comes out to win and
to play hard every night. If
you are going to be a good
defensive player, which he
is, then you have to have
that kind of tough, fierce
competitive edge about
you. And he has that along
with his other talents.

Nate Thurmond

One of the things I remember that really shows what Rick Barry was all about was the year we won the championship. In Game 7 at the Oakland Coliseum and Rick was 2-for-15 going into the fourth quarter. And I'll be darned if he didn't come out in that fourth quarter and make five straight shots and lead us to victory. That typifies what Rick Barry was all about.

Al Attles coached the Golden State Warriors and Rick Barry to the NBA title in 1975.

Hal Greer

The guy scored over 20,000 points and he epitomized what a pro is supposed to be.

He'd wear a thigh pad, he wore a knee brace, he had both ankles taped, he had a bandage on his arm, but he was always there. He had as great a 15- to 17-foot jump shot as anyone who's ever played the game. It was so good in fact that he used to shoot foul shots by shooting a jump shot. He was tough and he was a smart cookie.

Billy Cunningham, teammate of Hal Greer on the 1967 NBA champion Philadelphia 76ers.

I remember when he came into the ABA as a 19-year-old. He was just a tall, skinny kid. We all thought, 'Who does this skinny kid think he is?' But when he started to fill out it was easy to see how great he was going to become because he just kept working at his game. He was my least favorite center to go against, of all time, and that includes Kareem. I could always take Kareem outside and either shoot over him or drive by. But I hated to go against Moses. Any advantage you had against other centers, he was able to negate because of his quickness. And he was just relentless getting to the basketball. He just never stopped working.

Dan Issel on Moses Malone, who averaged 18.8 points and 14.6 rebounds as a
19-year-old rookie with the ABA's Utah Stars in 1974-75.

Moses

The size, the talent and his persistency is what made Elvin Hayes the player he was. He's still the prototype power forward, the guy with the body who can run and rebound. Every night you could count on 20 points, 12 rebounds, two or three blocked shots. Every night, even on bad nights. He's still got to be the prototype when somebody's looking for an NBA power forward.

Denver Nuggets general manager Bernie Bickerstaff was an assistant coach with the Washington Bullets for 11 seasons. Elvin Hayes, who missed only nine games in his 16 years, scored 27,313 points and grabbed 16,279 rebounds from 1968 to 1984, most of those during his nine seasons with the Bullets.

I think the time I played was a great part of the formation of the NBA. We tried to play with dignity. We always played hard. And we tried to represent the league on a top-notch basis. So our era was very important. It was the formation of what the game is today.   George Mikan had six of the first seven 50-point games in the NBA history. He played for nine years between 1946 and 1956.

Dave just wanted to win.

And he played so hard that he wouldn't accept any less from anybody around him. If a guy was sloughing off or slacking in any manner, Dave Cowens would let him know in no uncertain terms. He was only about 6-feet-9, but he was a dominant center. He just played so fierce. I remember Bob Lanier telling me one time after he had played against Dave, 'Dave is nuts. I mean, he's just crazy.' But that's the way Dave Cowens played.

Paul Silas, teammate of Dave Cowens who helped lead Boston to NBA titles in 1974 and 1976.

Julius

was a fierce competitor like all great players. People might not have noticed that on a regular basis because of the way he conducted himself. He always appeared to be very much under control, which he was. But the one thing you knew coaching him was if he had a bad night the night before, you knew he was going to be ready the next night. He could not stand that. If you look at greatness there is one quality all these people have. They're always striving for perfection even though they know they'll never achieve that. Julius Erving was no different.

Hall of Fame forward Billy Cunningham coached the Philadelphia 76ers and Julius Erving, whose dramatic play turned the team into one of the NBA's greatest road shows in the late 1970s and early 1980s.

CHARLES IS A SHOWMAN. Once it was show time, once it was time to start the game, Charles was all business. But he also had a sense of responsibility to entertain people. And just by the very nature and style of his game, Charles was entertaining. He loved to jaw with referees. He loved to jaw with

other players. And he liked to have fun with the mascots and everything around the game. Charles was not a tunnel vision kind of guy. He is some-body who looks around, sees what's there, and drinks everything in. And he wants to make sure everybody's had a good time. Matt Guokas coached Charles Barkley for 2¹/₂ seasons with the Philadelphia 76ers.

For 48 minutes you and I were going to knock heads. If you had something weak about you, then I was going to exploit it and make it weaker.

Wes Unseld, a 6-foot-7 center, became the only player to be named Rookie of the Year and Most Valuable Player in the same season when he averaged 13.8 points and 18.2 rebounds for the Baltimore Bullets in 1968-69.

DeBusschere

had a tremendous amount of knowledge of the game. He had been a player-coach in Detroit and he brought a level of maturity, a sincerity, a vision. Those New York Knicks teams became better on the perimeter because DeBusschere was able to shoot the ball. We became a better ball-handling team because he could pass and make the play. He was a ferocious rebounder for his size. And he was very competitive. He played to win and he understood how the game was played.

Willis Reed on Dave DeBusschere. DeBusschere was a player-coach at age 24 and a major league pitcher for the Chicago White Sox during his 12-year NBA career.

Michael Jordan is the greatest competitor in the history of sports, not just basketball.

This guy is an

assassin

in shorts.

When Michael Jordan's playing days are over the CIA should enlist him to take out anybody they find objectionable or possibly damage the country's security.

He is the ultimate competitor.

Jack Ramsay was an NBA head coach for 21 years from 1968 to 1989.

706
consecutive games

Dolph was an intense competitor. And he never stopped running, never stopped

trying. I don't know what his heartbeat was but it had to be in the forties or high

thirties. He just had an immense amount of endurance. And he had a sensational

touch. He was just the kind of guy that one way or another would beat you.

Six-time NBA All-Star George Yardley on Dolph Schayes, who played in
706 straight games during his 16-year career from 1948 to 1964.

Tiny.

Nobody moves a team like

Even compared to the Tiny Archibald who led the league

in scoring and assists for me one year, which no one else

has ever done. This guy became a far, far more complete

player. Tiny had it all: instinct, vision, and, most impor-

tant, attitude — the unselfishness to give up the ball,

Bob Cousy, a 13-time All-Star point guard for the Boston Celtics,
coached Nate "Tiny" Archibald for four seasons including the 1972-73
season when Archibald became the only player to lead the league in
scoring (34.0) and assists (11.4).

The **greatest competitor** I think I've ever seen. I don't care what you're playing, **he wants to win**. And he's a very special person going down to the wire. We always went to **Jerry West** for the last shot because we knew he was going to make it. His nickname was **Mr. Clutch** and he carried that moniker well because every time we were in that situation, boom, he'd make the shot.

Jerry West?

I'll never forget the 1972 **All-Star Game**. He and Oscar Robertson were the guards. The score was tied with **seconds left** and Oscar took the ball out of bounds. He threw it to West, Jerry took **one dribble**, top of the key, bam! **Jump shot, game's over**, West wins the game. He did it at All-Star Games, he did it with the Lakers and he did it in college. And he was a great defensive player. **Just a great all-around player.**

"Hot" Rod Hundley preceded Jerry West at the University of West Virginia
where West broke all Hundley's records except one — shot attempts.

20,880

career points scored

Bob Pettit was the consummate pro. He could play in any era because he came to play every night. He was tenacious and an excellent rebounder. I mean, he really went after the ball. He had great anticipation and timing. And if you got the ball into his area he'd score. But the thing I was impressed with was that he was a professional on and off the court. And that was something that as a young player I was very impressed with. He never let any kind of distraction bother him. When Bob stepped onto the floor he was ready to play.

Rookie point guard Lenny Wilkens helped lead Bob Pettit and the St. Louis Hawks to the 1960 NBA Finals.

Jerry Lucas had probably the best knowledge of rebounding, scientifically, of any player I ever played with. I had never known a player to be so scientific about rebounding until I met Jerry Lucas. Nate Thurmond

George Gervin was the Iceman because he was always so cool and so unrattled. In our scouting reports before the game, we would say we were going to rattle him. We're going to play him tough and beat him up a little bit physically. But he would absorb all the punishment and keep smiling all along the way. He'd have 30 at halftime and you'd say, 'This is not working,' so then you'd start smiling along with him. Then he's got 40 and you're like, 'Wait a minute, we're losing this game.' That's the Iceman.

Spencer Haywood on Gerge Gervin. In 1970 Haywood successfully sued to become the first underclassman allowed to play in the NBA.

27.1

points per game

He was awesome and he had such great leadership that he could draw the team together with his scoring or his passing. I remember him gliding to the hoop and slamming over Kareem, slamming it over Nate Thurmond, or catching them up in the air and dishing the ball off. He could do everything for a guard. He's a legend.

Bob Lanier on Dave Bing, who averaged 27.1 points during the 1967-68 season to lead the NBA in scoring.

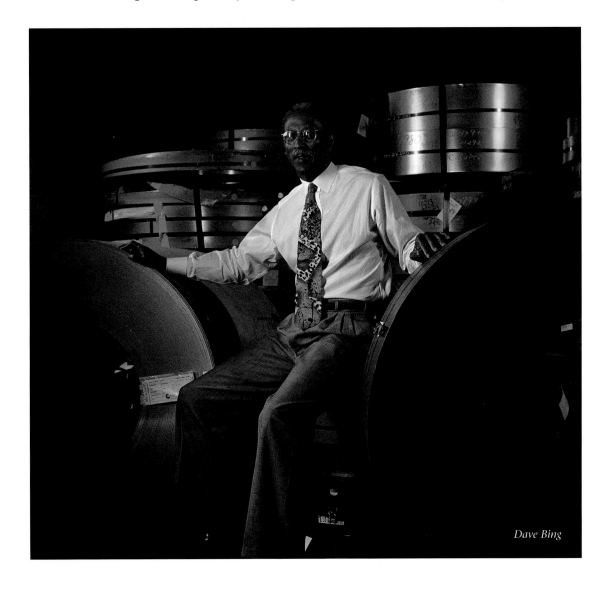

Dave Bing

"Havlicek steals the ball!"

He was like the bionic man. People at Harvard were doing studies on his heart rate because he appeared to have this great stamina because he never stopped running. But John Havlicek was a great scorer and a great competitor. He was a winner in every sense of the word. He loved the pressure situation and he loved to come through, particularly on defense. He's one of the all-time great defensive players.

Tom Heinsohn on John Havlicek. Together they helped Boston win three championships from 1962 through 1965.

Bill was the most disciplined person I've ever seen. On the court, he never took a bad shot. Never. He was in constant motion, running the court in a circle and running his man into picks. Eventually, he either ran his man into the ground or wiped him out on a pick, and he was open. Then, his shot was automatic.

Bob Cousy delivered a good portion of his 6,955 career assists to Bill Sharman. In addition to being one of the greatest free-throw shooters in league history, Sharman coached the 1971-72 Los Angeles Lakers to a 69-13 record, the second best in NBA history.

Bill Sharman

1,014

all-time career wins

As a point guard, being a player-coach came easy to me because I knew who should have the ball, who had a hot hand and who we should go to. I was successful at it. My last year at Seattle as a player-coach, we won 47 games. It wasn't until I was player-coach in Portland during the 1974-75 season that I knew the tide was starting to change and it was too difficult to do both. There was a lot more pressing and double-teaming in the game. I could make a pass into the low post, but I saw guys who couldn't. I knew I had to do more teaching and more coaching. I realized the game was changing quickly, and that at the end of the year I was going to have to go in one direction. So I went into coaching.

Lenny Wilkens was a nine-time All-Star before turning to coaching where he has become the league's all-time leader in victories with 1,014 through the 1995-96 season.

He's a winner and that's what makes him special.
He just knows how to win. He wants to win and

he will do anything to win.

That's Larry Bird in a nutshell.
He was one of the smartest players to ever play the game.
Just the Bird Man, that's all.

Earvin "Magic" Johnson

The NBA was a dream come true for me.

I grew up in a non-athletic family where my parents were interested in music, literature, education and art. I remember when I was in the seventh grade, my parents, who worked all the time, would give up their weekends to drive me to these stupid little basketball games that I was so interested in playing in. And I was sitting there as a seventh grader, and I looked over at my dad as he was driving along wishing he could be home listening to Mozart, and I said, 'Dad, one day I'm going to win the MVP in the NBA, and for winning the MVP you get a brand new car and I'm going to give you that car, Dad.' And my dad looked back at me and said, 'What's the NBA?' My dad still has that car and I'm very proud of that.

Bill Walton led Portland to the 1977 NBA title, and a year later, despite playing just 58 games due to career-threatening foot injuries, averaged 18.9 points, 13.2 rebounds, 5.0 assists and 2.52 blocked shots as the Trail Blazers bolted to a 50-8 record. Portland finished 8-16 without him.

Robert reminded me of Bill Russell. In addition to having the same great pride, the man was totally involved in doing the things that help win ballgames.

K.C. Jones, the fifth former Boston player to take over the Celtics head coaching job, helped Robert Parish and Boston to the Finals four times in his five seasons from 1983 to 1988.

61

Elgin Baylor scored an NBA Finals record 61 points at Boston to put the Los Angeles Lakers up 3-2 against the eventual champion Celtics in 1962.

He was without a doubt, for many years, the most unique player I'd ever seen. People talk about today's modern players. He was one of the first modern players. He was one of the first players that had that incredible ability and that incredible knack to not only do the right thing, but the most spectacular thing. This guy was a magician around the basket. And he was only 6-feet-5. But he was blessed with a great physical package, with great strength and huge hands. He had the ability to maneuver the basketball around people. He was also an incredible rebounder for his size. He had a unique magic.

Jerry West on Elgin Baylor. West and Baylor played 12 years together with the Los Angeles Lakers and four times were named to the All-NBA First Team in the same season.

This guy had unbelievable strength. And he was a tremendous athlete. He could run, he could jump and he just towered over most of the people in the league. He was just a great threat at both ends of the floor. I remember one time playing against Wilt in Philadelphia. We played at the War Memorial Stadium. And we went across

the street to a restaurant after the game. One of my friends was the bartender and he said, 'Red, how did you do against Chamberlain?' I said, 'I got 38 points.' He says, 'Set 'em up, my boy got 38 points.' And as he's setting 'em up he says, 'How did Wilt do?' I said, 'He got 63.' I mean, that's the kind of thing Wilt could do to you.

Johnny "Red" Kerr and Wilt Chamberlain were teammates in Philadelphia during a portion of the 1964-65 season.

When I first came to the University of Houston, so many things were happening. I was new to everything. I didn't know who was who. Everybody was talking about Michael Young because he was the high school All-American. But Clyde was a bigger surprise. From the first day as a freshman, he was outstanding. So winning the championship together with the Houston Rockets was the ultimate. To come back together, the two of us, and to win a championship, that was a great moment that I'll never forget.

Hakeem Olajuwon and Clyde Drexler played together at the University of Houston.
Drexler was traded to the Rockets midway through Houston's second NBA championship run in 1995.

the first quadruple double

Nate Thurmond was an unsung hero. He probably had the best timing,
even as good as Bill Russell's timing was. Nate was great at closing up the hoop.

Bob Lanier

In those days we had scoring forwards and defensive forwards. **Paul Arizin** and I were scoring forwards so we rarely guarded one another. But I remember guarding Paul for one half when Alex Hannum was my coach. Paul had a great jump shot, a line drive kind of shot, but believe me, it always went in. So he scored 22 points on me, and at half-time Alex said, 'I thought I told you to watch him.' And I said, 'I was watching him, and man, can he shoot!'

Dolph Schayes on Paul Arizin, who was an All-Star in every one of his ten seasons from 1950-51 to 1961-62 except the two he missed early in his career because of military service.

Kevin McHale

You always knew what you were going

to get from Kevin, and you could depend on it.

There were times when Larry Bird was off and times

when Robert Parish was off, but there were very few

times Kevin was off, and if he was, it meant he'd shoot

only 48 percent, instead of 58 percent.

M.L. Carr and Kevin McHale were teammates in Boston from 1980 to 1985.

If you asked a lot of people around the league who they would start a team with, I would say David, Shaquille O'Neal and Grant Hill, not in any particular order, would be the names you'd hear. David is truly as good as any player in the league, and as well respected as any player in the league. Based on my experience with him, I would love to coach that guy again. I would take my chances with David any day. He's always going to put you in position to win a championship.

Larry Brown, head coach of the Indiana Pacers, was David Robinson's first professional coach at San Antonio where the Spurs improved from 21 victories the year before Robinson's arrival to 56 and the Midwest Division championship in 1989-90.

david robinson

JOHN STOCKTON

I think it's a great thing, always having my name linked with his. He's like me in so many ways: We don't like missing practice, we don't like missing games. Talent is fine, but you've got to have the desire to want to do it every night, to get here at 8:30 in the morning, spend that time in the weight room. But you don't just get a work ethic. You've got to come with it. I think John was born with it.

Karl Malone on John Stockton, who has won a record nine straight assists titles. The pair have missed four games each out of a combined 1,886 since they entered the NBA in 1985 and 1984, respectively.

Vhen Karl Malone is challenged, he is at his best. We were going into a city one time and John Stockton was getting

on him because a player on another team said Karl was overrated. Karl didn't say much, but he went out and got more

than 50 points that night.

Jerry Sloan, one of the great defensive guards in NBA history, has been an assistant or the head coach during Karl Malone's 11 seasons with the Utah Jazz.

I'm a man with many talents. I'm just following my dreams and taking advantage of opportunities that come my way. I'm a basketball player slash entertainer. Basketball is entertainment. People pay money to come see you dunk, sweat, dive on the floor. And they come to see you make faces, trash talk. They come to see you do a lot of things.

Shaquille O'Neal entered the NBA at 20, published his autobiography at 21, made his first rap album at 22, won the NBA scoring title at 23, and starred in his first feature film at 24.

I turned the corner in a game against the Washington Bullets in 1978 and got around whoever was guarding me. I went up in the air with one hand and I remember Elvin Hayes coming from the weak side. He went up with two hands and he was looking at me. I could feel his presence. My momentum carried me forward and I just threw the ball down. That it was Elvin, probably made it more special. **I just ran down the court like nothing happened, but I knew something very serious had just taken place.**

Julius "Dr. J" Erving

SHOW TIME

He was the most unbelievable center to ever play the game in terms of domination and intimidation. There have been a lot of players that have played as well at different positions, but there's no one that's ever played the game any better than Wilt Chamberlain. I played with him and I played against him. He was just unique. There's not a center playing today that could stop Wilt Chamberlain from scoring. If he played in the league when he was 26 or 27 years old, he would lead the league in scoring, he would lead the league in rebounding, he would lead the league in blocked shots. This was a man for all ages.

Jerry West played with and against Wilt Chamberlain from 1960 to 1973.

big men

George was big. He had shoulders probably wider than any center currently playing in the NBA. It's just a good thing George Mikan had a good nature because everybody tried to pressure him and get him out of his position around the basket. But he had tremendous desire to excel. He was a great rebounder as well. I think he could have played today.

Harry "The Horse" Gallatin averaged 10 or more rebounds a game during 9 of his 10 NBA seasons from 1948 to 1957-58.

I think there will be a period of orientation for me like there is for every newcomer in the NBA, but I think in the long run I'll be able to handle myself man-to-man with anyone in the league.

Wilt Chamberlain, October 1959

99
The next highest Lakers uniform number was 34.

12
On March 7, 1954, Mikan's Lakers beat Milwaukee 65-63 in a game played with a 12-foot basket.

5
Mikan's Lakers won five championships between 1949 and 1954.

4
Prior to the 24-second clock, there were seven 50-point games. Mikan had four of them.

2
At least two rules were changed as a result of Mikan's dominance. Goaltending, permitted in the early years, was outlawed and in 1951 the lane was widened from six feet to twelve feet.

I used to like to keep my hands on my hips. As a result, it made me wider. They'd have to go around an elbow. **And a lot of times I could effectively use that elbow to deter them from coming around by giving 'em a whack.** Paul Seymour was playing me in Syracuse because all the other centers, Mike Novak and a couple of the other guys, had fouled out. They wound up using Seymour to guard me in the center lane. He comes in and he starts pinching me behind the legs. And I said, 'Paul, you better cut that out because I don't like it.' And he started putting his finger in my face and ridiculing me. So I set it up with the guys to throw me a pass at just the right height. I throw a fake at Paul and come around with a high elbow. **And I hit him right between the eyes with that elbow and went in and scored the basket.** Of course, the official called a foul against him. And there was a lot of discussion about that. It was sort of funny to watch Paul because as he talked, arguing the play to the officials, a big lump came out. He looked like he was a unicorn. And about that time my teammate, Billy Hassett, comes up to him and says, 'What are you yelling about Paul?' Paul took a swing at him and said, 'I can handle you.' So, he gave him a good shot.

George Mikan was listed at 6-feet-10 and weighed 245 pounds.

Bill Russell and Wilt Chamberlain

Bill Russell took defensive basketball and made it an art form. He never went up before the ball was released and he would cut down the angle to the point that the offensive player couldn't use the other side of the basket. In other words, Russell would pick him off with the net.   Tom Heinsohn

Was it important to dominate? Yes.
One thing you want to do to your opponent is make them know they can't win. Never let them gain their confidence or think that anything is going to be easy. Sometimes the anticipation is more than enough to offset their ability.

Bill Russell

He was a man playing with boys.
Wilt had his nights against him, but even Wilt developed that little fallaway shot because he couldn't get the ball into the basket against Russ. If Wilt tried to overpower him, Russ's speed and quickness would just neutralize it. I don't remember anyone else having even marginal success against Bill Russell.

Bob Cousy

There is no question in my mind that I have never seen, even to this day, a better center than Bill Russell.

Red Auerbach

Russell didn't want to give you a shot if you were underneath the basket. He didn't want to give you a shot if you were 15 feet away. He didn't want to give you a shot if you were 20 feet away. He had this great desire and pride to stop you and instincts that were amazing.   Johnny "Red" Kerr

The original 24-second clock was a floor model and made its debut October 30, 1954.

24-second shot clock

The game had become a stalling game. A team would get ahead, even in the first half, and it would go into a stall. The other team would keep fouling and it got to be a constant parade to the foul line. In 1952 we played a game in which neither team took a shot in the last eight minutes. Coaches will take advantage of anything to win. If they can win a game 3-2, that's okay with them. And you can't blame them — that's why they're getting paid. But if you're a promoter, that won't do. We needed a time element in our game. The number of seconds wasn't important.

Danny Biasone, owner of the Syracuse Nationals, invented the 24-second clock in 1954.

DANNY BIASONE'S
24-second Formula

Take the length of the game,
48 minutes or 2,880 seconds.

2,880

Divide by average number
of shots in a game.

120

2,880 ÷ 120 = 24

Answer:

24

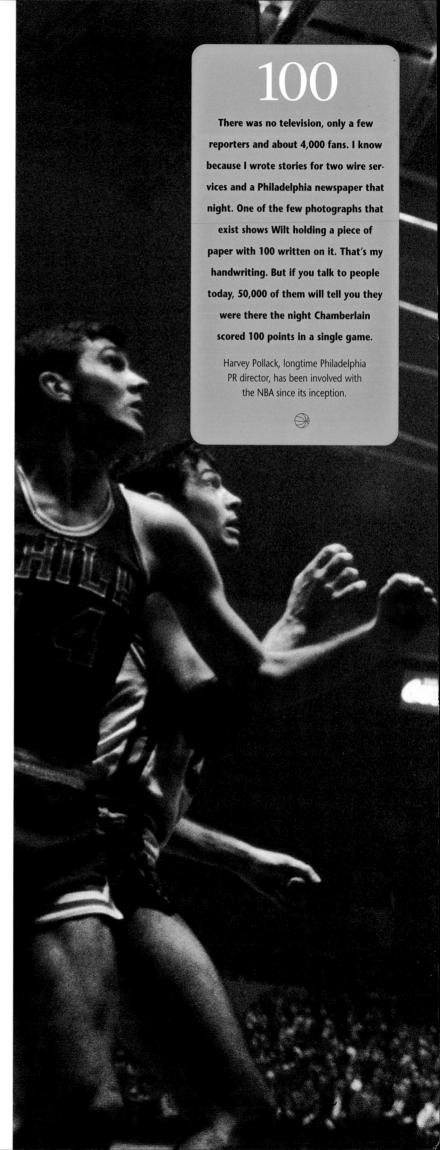

Since it was near the end of the season and our place in the standings was interchangeable for the playoffs, I took some time to enjoy myself the night before the game. I was playing for the Philadelphia Warriors, but I lived in New York City. I had to be in Philly by 1:00 p.m. that day to catch the team bus for Hershey, Pennsylvania, where we were actually playing the game. I had absolutely no sleep the night before. I didn't sleep on the train, afraid I might miss my stop and end up in Washington, D.C. On the bus ride from Philadelphia to Hershey, about a two-hour trip, I spent the whole time talking to my best friend, Vince Miller. We arrived at the arena in Hershey at 3:30 p.m. and I spent the rest of the time before the game shooting a rifle at a penny arcade. I completely destroyed all existing shooting records there — an omen of things to come.

A career .511 shooter from the foul line, Wilt Chamberlain connected on 28 of 32, including 24 of his first 25 against the New York Knicks on March 2, 1962.

100

There was no television, only a few reporters and about 4,000 fans. I know because I wrote stories for two wire services and a Philadelphia newspaper that night. One of the few photographs that exist shows Wilt holding a piece of paper with 100 written on it. That's my handwriting. But if you talk to people today, 50,000 of them will tell you they were there the night Chamberlain scored 100 points in a single game.

Harvey Pollack, longtime Philadelphia PR director, has been involved with the NBA since its inception.

March 2, 1962 at Hershey, Pa.

PHILADELPHIA WARRIORS

Player	POS.	FGM	FGA	FTM	FTA	PTS.
Paul Arizin	F	7	18	2	2	16
Tom Meschery	F	7	12	2	2	16
Wilt Chamberlain	C	36	63	28	32	100
Guy Rodgers	G	1	4	9	12	11
Al Attles	G	8	8	1	1	17
York Larese		4	5	1	1	9
Ed Conlin		0	4	0	0	0
Joe Ruklick		0	1	0	2	0
Ted Luckenbill		0	0	0	0	0
Totals		63	11	43	52	169

When I came into the league, Bill Russell and Wilt Chamberlain were the top two centers and they wore beards. I wore a beard, too. I was always right there with them. But I was on the West Coast where we weren't drawing a lot of people. Then, when

I thought I was ready to ascend to be the best center in the league, along comes Kareem Abdul-Jabbar. That's why I played so hard against Kareem. I wanted that position he inherited. Nate Thurmond began his 14-year career with San Francisco in 1963.

don't think I ever saw this guy not do anything that was asked of him or beg out of a practice. Never once. He went to practice and he

practiced like the 11th or 12th man. He showed up for every basketball game. He competed in every basketball game. But I think the most

remarkable thing about him is here's a man who played for 20 years. He came into this league at a time when basketball was just growing.

He left this game when the league was at its height of popularity. During that course of time he played against some people who were in the

Hall of Fame and he played against today's young lions. And I don't think he saw anyone who scared him. He taught a lot of lessons to a

lot of young centers in this league. People are going to look back and say what an incredible feat it was to play in the NBA for 20 years.

This is hard work. This is not like some sports where you can walk around at times or have a lot of time off between plays. This is a grueling,

demanding, physical sport.

Jerry West, who played against Kareem Abdul-Jabbar in the early 1970s, coached him for three years in the late 1970s,
and then built five championship teams around him in the 1980s as the Los Angeles Lakers' general manager.

Kareem Abdul-Jabbar

He was so good at an early age. When he came into the league he didn't look like he was a rookie. He played like a veteran and his skill level was so high. The little things he did, like his wonderful ability to handle the basketball. Plus, he had great size. He had the ability to play the game and he knew situations and how to make plays. Those things I marveled at those first few years. I played like a rookie my first year, Oscar did not.

Jerry West on Oscar Robertson. West and Robertson occupied the guard spots on the All-NBA First Team for six straight seasons from 1962 to 1967.

30.8 points, 12.5 rebounds, 11.4 assists — Oscar Robertson, 1961-62.

Oscar was the best player I ever played against.
The guy did not have a weakness. The term

"triple double"

is something that comes up frequently today and
it's a big deal when somebody gets one.
Oscar averaged a triple double for one season
and almost three or four others.
When you have a player of that caliber,
you say to yourself, 'How do I stop him?'
He was such a powerful player and had
such great control that he could move whoever
was guarding him all over the floor.
There's nothing Oscar Robertson couldn't do.

John Havlicek

Bob Cousy
Bill Sharman
Bill Russell
Tom Heinsohn
John Havlicek
Sam Jones

RED AUERBACH

K.C. Jones
Satch Sanders
Dave Cowens
Larry Bird
Robert Parish
Kevin McHale

I didn't treat everybody the same. But I didn't have double standards. In other words, given the temperament of certain people, you never bawl them out. You never give them hell. You talk to them. For example, Cousy. You talk to him. K.C. Jones, you talk to. Heinsohn, you'd get on his tail, see. Russell, you'd get on his tail every once in a while

because he'd get careless. But everybody had a different personality. I never bawled out Havlicek. I don't believe I ever bawled out Ramsey. And one other thing, I never cussed a player. Not that I was Casper Milquetoast. Sure I cussed. But I never cussed out one of my players. And I never blamed a player when we lost a ballgame. Never!

Red Auerbach coached the Boston Celtics to nine championships in 10 years between 1957 and 1966.

Bob Cousy In 1950, Celtics picked his name out of a hat after Chicago Stags franchise folded. Eight-time assist champion, 13-time All-Star, 10-time All-NBA First Team.

Bill Sharman Another one of Auerbach's trades t░░░d dividends for nearly a decade. Acquir░░in a 1951 deal with the Ft. Wayne Pistons░░ing free-throw shooter seven times, eight-time All-Star, and later became known as one of the most innovative coaches in league history with the Los Angeles Lakers where he won one championship (1972).

Bill Russell One of the great trades in the history of team sports. The Celtics dealt All-Star Ed Macauley and future All-Star Cliff Hagan to St. Louis for Russell's draft rights in 1956. Played and later coached Celtics to 11 titles in 13 years.

Tom Heinsohn Territorial pick in the 1956 NBA Draft. Solid scorer and rebounder, Heinsohn played on eight title teams and later coached the Celtics to championships in 1974 and 1976.

Sam Jones First-round pick, eighth overall, in 195░ NBA Draft. Played on 10 title teams, one of the first great shooting guards.

K.C. Jones Second-round pick in the 1956 NBA Draft. One of the most successful athletes in the history of sports. Won Olympic Gold Medal in 1956, played on two NCAA championship teams, eight-time champion with the Celtics and later coached Boston to three titles in the 1980s.

John Havlicek First-round pick in the 1962 NBA Draft, seventh overall. One of the great all-around forwards in the history of the game, seventh-round pick by the Cleveland Browns. Played on eight title teams in 16 years and scored more than 26,000 points.

Satch Sanders First-round pick in 1960 NBA Draft, seventh overall. Defensive stopper and solid all-around contributor during 13 seasons and eight championships.

Larry Bird Selected as a junior, eligible under a rule that was later changed, Bird made Boston one of the NBA's most dominant teams in the 1980s. Boston took Bird with the No. 6 choice in the 1978 Draft but had to wait an entire year as Bird chose to finish his college career before joining the Celtics.

Robert Parish and Kevin McHale One of Auerbach's greatest moves landed Parish and McHale in the same deal. Boston dealt two 1980 first-round draft choices to Golden State for Parish and the Warriors' first-round pick in the 1980 Draft, No. 3 overall, which the Celtics used to select McHale.

I was at a golf tournament and someone came up to Bill Russell and asked him what he thought about the Chicago Bulls three-peating. And he said, 'Not much.' And it wasn't any disrespect, but the Celtics won 8 in a row, 9 out of 10, 11 out of 13. When you try to measure someone up to those numbers, you look at other accomplishments a little differently.

John Havlicek

Jerry West's 1985 NBA Championship ring.

There were numerous times during my career I wanted to say,

'Enough's enough.'

I didn't want to play basketball anymore. I always felt that when you give and go above and beyond maybe what other people do, you're supposed to be rewarded. I was rewarded with contracts that paid me money. But I wasn't rewarded with what I really wanted. I wanted to win a championship and I really didn't think that was ever going to happen, because on the two occasions when we should have won, we didn't. And it was so frustrating to listen to the other locker room and see the incredible amount of attention that goes with winning, the wonderful feeling that you have after a summer of hard work. None of that was there. Then to come back to training camp and think, 'Are we going to get in a position to win again?' All those things became very frustrating. Consequently, every game against the Celtics during the regular season was like a championship game. That was the time you tried to work off your frustration. You wanted to beat those people.

Jerry West never beat Boston in the playoffs during his playing days, but as the Lakers'
general manager, Los Angeles upended the Celtics in the 1985 and 1987 Finals.

Jerry West and John Havlicek

I roomed with Chuck Cooper for a portion of my first season. We were both rookies in 1950. I remember we had an exhibition game in Charlotte and Chuck wasn't allowed to stay in the same hotel. He couldn't even eat in the same places. Now I came out of New York and went to school in New England. Chuck was educated in Pittsburgh, a fairly large and sophisticated city. And Chuck was a very bright and sensitive guy. He never said anything, but I could tell. He had never really been hit in the face with it before. I guess I was aware of nasty people and bigots out there, but I looked at what was happening and I was embarrassed to be white. He and I went to Arnold and said, 'This is crazy. If you don't mind we're going to get out of here. We don't want to stay in this town any more than we have to.' Arnold gave us permission and we went to catch a midnight train so Chuck wouldn't have to worry about a place to stay. We go to the train station and I had never seen a Black-White sign for a men's room. Here we are standing there. This guy has become a good friend and he's my teammate. I'm so embarrassed I don't know what to say to the man. We want to use the restroom and he's got to go one way and I have to go the other. I thought we had landed on another planet. We were able to show that kind of support for Chuck. But I don't know if we demonstrated that enough for Russell. I never discussed that with him and I don't know how he feels about it, but there's no question that today I would do that. Maybe we were just afraid to make a statement in those days. But it should have been done.

Red Auerbach never considered the consequences of selecting Duquesne star Chuck Cooper in the 1950 NBA Draft. Auerbach needed players and Cooper could play.

"When I looked at players, I didn't look to see what color they were," says Auerbach. "What did I care? I was trying to build a team and Cooper was a good prospect."

Boston used a second-round pick on Cooper, making him the first African-American player ever selected in the NBA Draft. Washington later took Earl Lloyd in the eighth round. Nat "Sweetwater" Clifton, who had been playing for the Globetrotters, became the first player to sign while Lloyd has the distinction of being the first player to appear in an NBA game. Don Barksdale, who came into the league a year later with Baltimore, was the first African–American player to appear in an All-Star Game (1953).

Meanwhile, Auerbach's Celtics remained years ahead of the rest of society. In the mid 1960s Boston was the first team to start five African-Americans and in 1966 Auerbach turned the head coaching duties over to legendary Bill Russell, the NBA's first African-American head coach.

Bob Cousy was the first great player for Red Auerbach's Celtics, eventually leading them to six championships during his 13 seasons with Boston from 1950 to 1963.

Chuck Cooper with Red Auerbach

If you look at the early days, there were not a lot of blacks. A lot of blacks who were great players didn't make teams because they didn't want too many. You always heard those things. We played an exhibition game in Lubbock, Texas, and we stayed in a Holiday Inn. Lo and behold, we got there and they put us in a little section and pulled a huge curtain across the room. Maybe I was overly sensitive, maybe I wasn't. But I said, 'If you don't move the curtain, I'm not going to play.' There was no reason for that curtain. There was hardly anyone in the restaurant. They did it because there were blacks on our team. If you talk to other guys, they were going through the same thing in the '60s.

Spencer Haywood averaged 19.2 points and 9.3 rebounds in 12 NBA seasons from 1970 to 1983.

Wilt Chamberlain		Best of the Rest
45.8	45.8 **career** average minutes per game	Nate Archibald is the last player to average 45 minutes for **one season** (1972-73)
47	47 consecutive complete games	A.C. Green has 7 **career** complete games
1,700	1,700 or more rebounds 10 straight years	No player on a 1995-96 NBA roster ever had more than 1,530 in **one season**
3	Top three highest scoring games in NBA history	David Robinson is the only other center in top 35
22.9	22.9 career rebounds per game	Dennis Rodman averaged less than 13 rebounds through his first 10 seasons
56	56 NBA regular season records	Michael Jordan has 4
55	55 rebounds in one game	1995-96 Chicago Bulls had 55 rebounds in a game only twice
14	14 games with 40 or more rebounds	No player on a 1995-96 NBA roster ever had as many as 36
48.5	averaged 48.5 minutes per game one season	Archibald ranks eighth (46.0) and is only player other than Wilt in top 10
50	50 or more points 45 times in one season	Jordan has 27 **career** 50-point games

THINGS JUST INSTINCTIVELY CAME TO ME AND I KNEW HOW TO REACT. But growing up in Washington, D.C., that was really the only outlet we had during the summer. Because when I grew up in Washington, D.C., the playgrounds were segregated. We didn't even have a place to play until I was 14 or 15 years old which is when I started playing ball. They built a park, or part of a park with a basketball court right around the corner from where I lived. So that's where our summers were spent. That part of the park was just for blacks. They had a white part of the park where blacks could not participate. They had tennis courts, swimming pools, baseball diamonds, football. And the only thing they had for the blacks was the basketball court. We could go to the other

side of the park, but we could only go at night. It closed at 9 o'clock and that's when we went. So that was it, basketball. And that's what we spent our entire days doing in the summer. I never saw anyone do some of the things I did. It's really nothing you practice. It's just something that happens as I'm sure Julius or Michael will tell you. The defense dictates what you're going to do offensively, what kind of shot you're going to take depending upon the predicament you're in. It's just something that's God-given with those guys and it was the same with me. The body control, the athletic ability to do that — is nothing you can practice because you don't know you can do them. It's more than the basics, the jump shot, drop step or moves you can work on. It just happens.

Elgin Baylor averaged 27.4 points and 13.5 rebounds and was named to the All-NBA First Team 10 times during his 14-year career between 1958 and 1972.

Elgin Baylor is still the premier quick forward in NBA history. I'm sure you would get an argument about Dr. J, Larry Bird and other players. But not only was he a great offensive player, rebounder and passer — which is evident in the record books — but of all the players that could be compared with Elgin, he was by far the best defensive player.

Tom Heinsohn played opposite Baylor for eight years during the great Celtics-Lakers rivalry of the late 1950s and 1960s.

The first thing you have to do is understand the value of thinking 'Miss.' No matter where a shot is taken or who is taking that shot, you have to think the shooter is going to miss. It doesn't matter if the player is a good shooter or a bad shooter. To be a great rebounder you have to be thinking about a missed shot anytime one is taken. When a shot is taken on one side of the basket, seven out of ten times it comes off on the other side.

Wes Unseld played from 1968 to 1981 and finished his career with more rebounds (13,769) than points (10,624).

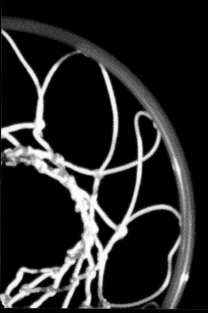

Dennis Rodman and Moses Malone are the only two players
to win as many as five consecutive rebounding titles.

Although Rodman's 18.7 average during the 1991-92 season
was the highest since Wilt Chamberlain's 19.2 in 1971-72, when
it comes to rebounds, Chamberlain, Bill Russell, Wes Unseld
and Jerry Lucas remain in a class of their own.

Chamberlain averaged 22.9 rebounds for his career and
six times averaged 24 or more during the regular season,
while also winning seven scoring championships. Russell averaged
22.5 including seven straight seasons when he averaged 23 or
more. Lucas is the only forward to average as many as
20 rebounds in a season and he did it two consecutive years.
He finished with a career average of 15.6 to go along with a
17-point scoring average. Unseld, who stood only 6-foot-7, played
center in an era that included Kareem Abdul-Jabbar, Chamberlain,
Russell and Nate Thurmond. He averaged 14.0 rebounds
during his 12-year career.

The brown ball was really hard to see on TV or even if you were sitting in the balcony. I wanted something to be the symbol of our league. We were the American Basketball Association. America's colors are red, white and blue. We were going to have a red, white and blue ball or I wasn't going to be commissioner.

George Mikan became the ABA's first commissioner in 1967.

Artis Gilmore of the Kentucky Colonels.

Larry Brown was Dean Smith's assistant at North Carolina and I was playing in Italy. Larry's in Dean's office, North Carolina is at the Final Four. He gets on the phone and says, **'Hey, do you want to play in this new league, the ABA?'** He said, 'You play, I'll play.' Boom! We decided to play. At the time, Marty Blake happened to call. He wanted Larry to play for the St. Louis Hawks in the NBA. He says, **'You stiffs aren't going to get anything from that league. It's a dead league.'** So, we flew down to New Orleans and they gave us a $5,000 bonus check. We ran to the bank, cashed 'em. They didn't bounce. We said, **'Hell, this is a great league.'** The guy that gave us the checks was our first general manager, Morton Downey, Jr., who had been a salesman for the American Can Company. He was a definite 'no hoper.' He lasted about three months. These teams had no money and this guy's giving out gold-plated season tickets.

Doug Moe played five seasons in the ABA and was Larry Brown's assistant coach at Denver for two seasons before four ABA teams joined the NBA in 1976. Moe's 1981-82 Denver Nuggets averaged 126.5 points a game, an NBA record.

Julius Erving

We had heard about Julius Erving and asked for a tape of him. We got this grainy black-and-white film of the UMass-North Carolina game in the NIT. The quality was so bad that you could hardly tell what was going on, but we saw enough of Julius to sign him after his junior year. Since we'd never seen him live before he wore a (Virginia) Squires uniform, we thought he'd be able to help us on the boards and we hoped he'd be able to score some. We had no idea what he'd become.

Johnny "Red" Kerr, a former NBA star, helped Virginia sign Julius Erving and George Gervin to their first professional contracts.

Bedlam!

I saw the whole Lakers team standing around staring at this man. When I saw that, when they stopped warming up, something told me we might have these guys. And Willis set the tempo. He made the first two shots, jumpers from 15 to 17 feet, and that was it. When he did that we said, 'The Captain's ready.' Half of Willis Reed was better than anything else we could have put out there. Before the game I remember Bill Bradley telling him, 'Hey, Willis, if you could only walk, man, that will be enough.' So, he provided the inspiration and I provided the devastation. I just let it happen. I just let the game come to me.

Walt Frazier had 36 points, 19 assists, seven rebounds and three steals in the Knicks' 113-99 victory in Game 7 of the 1970 NBA Finals.

Willis Reed

People ask me, "What was your biggest thrill? Winning the world championship of basketball or becoming a United States Senator?" Well, it's a great honor to be a United States Senator. But that gives you a chance to work 14 hours a day to prove that your constituents were right in sending you there in the first place. But when you're talking about a thrill, well, thrill is when you're standing at center court having won the world championship with your fists thrown in the air. And the chills going up and down your spine. And the knowledge of your face aching because you have a smile that won't stop. And you know that you're the best in the world. That's a thrill.

Sen. Bill Bradley was the starting small forward on New York Knicks championship teams in 1970 and 1973.

New York Knicks center and captain, Willis Reed, went down hard with a leg injury in Game 5 of the 1970 NBA Finals. The Knicks, utilizing a "3-2 offense," put 6-8 power forward Dave DeBusschere at center and held on to win. But without Reed, the Knicks were pounded 135-113 in Game 6 at Los Angeles. Laid out on a trainer's table in the Knicks Madison Square Garden dressing room hours before Game 7, not even Reed thought he'd be able to play. But moments before the opening tap, the Garden started to rumble. Out from the tunnel, his right leg heavily taped, Reed made one of the most dramatic appearances in NBA history. As he limped toward the court, the Garden faithful erupted. Players at both ends of the court stopped and watched. The Knicks looked at the Lakers. The Lakers looked at Reed. He would play. And the Knicks would not lose. Their stunning 113-99 victory gave New York its first professional basketball title.

When the Bullets and Knicks played it raised the level of everybody's performance to absolutely the best. We were playing a college-style game. The 24-second clock was fully utilized because the defense became just that much more intense. I think because the matchups were all classics with (Wes) Unseld and Willis (Reed), Earl (Monroe) and Walt Frazier, Kevin Loughery and Dick Barnett, and, of course, Gus Johnson and Dave DeBusschere, that was maybe the classic matchup of all time. Of course, Bill Bradley and me had our part in it. If I had butterflies three hours before every game, then I had butterflies six hours before every game with the Knicks. That was very special.

Jack Marin played eleven NBA seasons from 1966 to 1977, six of those with the Bullets.

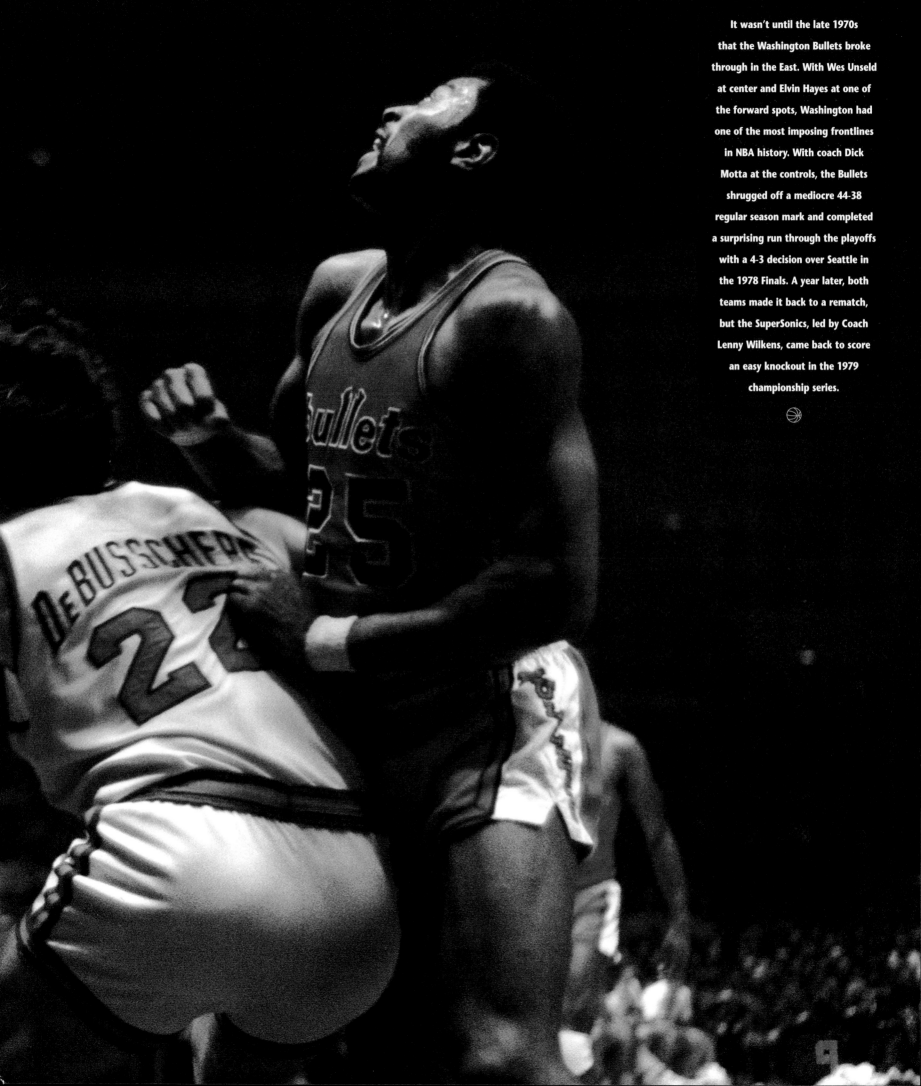

It wasn't until the late 1970s that the Washington Bullets broke through in the East. With Wes Unseld at center and Elvin Hayes at one of the forward spots, Washington had one of the most imposing frontlines in NBA history. With coach Dick Motta at the controls, the Bullets shrugged off a mediocre 44-38 regular season mark and completed a surprising run through the playoffs with a 4-3 decision over Seattle in the 1978 Finals. A year later, both teams made it back to a rematch, but the SuperSonics, led by Coach Lenny Wilkens, came back to score an easy knockout in the 1979 championship series.

individuality.

Walt Frazier played 13 seasons from 1967 to 1979. Frazier got the nickname "Clyde" when teammates saw him wearing the kind of wide-brimmed hat worn by Clyde in the movie, 'Bonnie and Clyde.'

Winning the championship in 1975 was an incredible accomplishment for the Golden State Warriors, especially the way it happened. It was like a fairy tale. We weren't even supposed to make the play-offs. Not only did we make the playoffs, we upset Chicago, who was supposed to defeat us in very dramatic fashion to win the Western Conference. Then we go onto the Finals where we were supposed to lose to Washington 4-0 and we end up beating them four straight. I think it is the most overlooked accomplishment in the history of professional sports on a championship level. I mean, people talk about the Jets in the Super Bowl, but they were supposed to win the AFL. We weren't even supposed to be in the NBA Playoffs and yet for only the third time to that point, a team lost in the Finals four games to nothing. You can talk about the New York Mets and what they did, but if you look back at the annals of the top professional sports, nothing compares to what we accomplished that season.

Rick Barry was named Finals MVP in 1975 after averaging 30.6 points and leading the league in steals and free-throw shooting (.904) during the 1974-75 regular season.

Our game style was predicated on excellent team play, fine timing, passing and cutting. The Sixers, because of their talent, had more of a one-on-one team. Julius Erving was marvelous with the ball. George McGinnis at the low-post was a strong guy who could score. And Doug Collins came at you from the edges. It was an outstanding team. But it was more a collection of stars than it was a highly integrated team. I don't think they could have played our style and we certainly wouldn't have any success playing theirs. It was just a situation where our style that year was good enough to win.   Jack Ramsay's teams made the playoffs 16 times during his 21-year NBA coaching career.

Doug Collins

It was sort of amazing because it was perceived as the individuals,

Philly, against the ultimate team, the Portland Trail Blazers. That's the way it was billed: The team versus the individual stars. You had myself, Julius, George McGinnis, Caldwell Jones, Steve Mix. Then you had Walton, Lucas, Lionel Hollins, Johnny Davis and Bobby Gross and Dave Twardzik. And we kicked hell out of them the first two games. The first one was close and the second game we beat them handily. But with three or four minutes to go, Darryl got into a fight with Bobby Gross and then Darryl and Lucas got into it. That changed the whole series. We never won a game after that. We fragmented. We did not pull together. Darryl was upset because he felt we let Maurice Lucas hit him from behind. He wasn't going to go to Portland. We had some guys complaining that they weren't getting to play. So here we are up 2-0 in the championship series and it was really our own internal strife that cost us. Portland hung together. They won Game 3 close, killed us in Game 4 and then broke through and won Game 5 in Philly. Then they won Game 6 by two. Everybody said, 'See, the team did beat the individuals.' But I went to Philly in 1973 to a team that had just finished 9-73, and four years later we were playing for a world championship. That doesn't just happen.

Doug Collins hit 55.7 percent of his shots and averaged 22.4 points for Philadelphia during the 1977 Playoffs.

That championship series was a perfect contrast between all the different elements in society and culture at that time. The individualism, the showmanship of the Sixers and the quiet, reserved teamwork of the Portland Trail Blazers. We had the ultimate respect for Philadelphia's talent. I don't really think they thought much about our team or our talent. But we had incredible physical talent that never was highlighted or exploited because it really wasn't the highwire act that Dr. J brought when he came in waving that ball behind his head as he came in for a vicious slam dunk with the big afro waving through the air. But the speed of the guards, the quickness of Bob Gross at small forward, the power of Maurice Lucas, the genius of Jack Ramsay. Yes, they had that great individual talent, but they had no concept of what it was like to play as a team.

Bill Walton averaged 18.2 points, 15.2 rebounds, 5.5 assists and blocked more than three shots a game during the 1977 postseason.

Dave Cowens

Bill Walton

Well, he came on the right side and we cut him off and there was no where for him to go but out of bounds. So, Julius said, 'If the only place I can go is out of bounds, then I'm gonna go out of bounds.' So he jumped in the air out of bounds. So now here he is walking through the air.

I thought he was going to pass out. Well, I guess I didn't know Julius as well as I thought I did. This man, out of bounds, floated from one side to the other.

I'm thinking, 'There's no way Doc can float all the way from this side of the hoop to the other side. We got him.'

Now, there's no way he can get a shot off, there's no angle there.

It kissed the glass and went in. Well, I guess he fooled me again. I looked at Coop (Michael Cooper) and he looked at me, and I said, 'Coop, you think we should ask him to do it again?' Now we're playing for the world championship. This is the fourth or fifth game and I could not believe my eyes because of the move this man had just made.

So he's got the ball and he's floating. And he spun it real high off the top of the glass.

And it's still the greatest move I've ever seen in basketball, the all-time greatest.

As a rookie, Earvin "Magic" Johnson replaced injured Kareem Abdul-Jabbar at center in Game 6 of the 1980 NBA Finals. Johnson scored 42 points and had 15 rebounds and seven assists to carry Los Angeles to the title over Julius Erving's Philadelphia 76ers.

Well, I pushed it out
think he'd be able

The tightest scoring race in NBA history didn't end until San Antonio's George Gervin, nearly exhausted and once more a champion, went to the bench in the third quarter of the last game of the 1978 regular season. Earlier in the day, Denver's David Thompson had scored 73 points by hitting 20 of his first 21 shots at Detroit. That night, however, Gervin won his fifth scoring title with a 68-point performance that included 53 in the first half, the second highest one half total in history.

ICE (George Gervin): I really didn't think I could.

SKYWALKER: I remember M.L. Carr saying, 'Well 'D', I think you got it. There's no way Gervin could get that many points.

ICE: A reporter called me at 3 o'clock in the afternoon and said, 'David just took your scoring title.'

SKYWALKER: We flew back to Denver from Detroit and I listened to San Antonio's game on the radio. But I stopped listening at halftime. Ice had 53.

ICE: Me and my teammates had a great relationship and they pushed me over the top.

SKYWALKER: Monte Towe called me and said, 'Well, you scored 73 points and that's a big accomplishment.' So, losing to a guy like Ice, there's no shame in that at all.

pretty far with 73. I didn't to catch me. David "Skywalker" Thompson

When you're on the free-throw line you're center stage. You have no one to blame but yourself. A lot of athletes don't like that pressure; they perform well when they're in a group because they have a reason why if things fall apart. I've always been a showoff. I've been a baton twirler since I was five years old and that's a solo situation. So I kind of like the center stage. I like people wondering, 'Is this little guy real?' I like the world looking at me.

Calvin Murphy hit 78 straight free throws during the 1980-81 season and his .892 career percentage ranks third all time.

Calvin Murphy, .958 highest percentage in one season.

Mark Price, .906 highest career free-throw percentage.

Rick Barry, .900 second highest career free-throw percentage.

Milwaukee's home floor at the Mecca complex was created in part by renowned pop artist Robert Indiana prior to the 1977-78 season. Indiana designed the art work that was painted onto the floor of the Milwaukee Arena. The colors were so bright the floor appeared to have an artificial surface, particularly to those watching Bucks games on television.

Michael epitomizes competitiveness. You always hear people talk about Michael's greatness, and what they see are his tremendous physical skills. But Michael's greatness is born from the fact he is the most fundamentally sound player in the NBA and he's the most mentally tough player in the NBA. When you put those things together and package them with that kind of physical ability, it's frightening. The thing I respect about Michael, amongst many other things, is that he never takes a night off. He realizes that when he plays it's just not good enough to be good. He has to be great. *Every night.* He has to find a way every night to be *great*. And the toll on him to live up to those standards, his standards, the level he created, I can't image what that must be like. Michael knows this. What he will be gauged against as he finishes his career are his own standards. The moment he starts to slip a little bit, it will be because of how great and phenomenal he has been. One thing about greatness is that those players are so demanding of themselves, so self-critical. A coach never has to demand a thing from Michael Jordan. That's the great thing about coaching Michael. His demands are far greater than any you could ever put on him. He's willing to put it on the line every single night.

Doug Collins was a four-time All-Star guard for Philadelphia in the 1970s before becoming head coach of the Chicago Bulls in 1986, Michael Jordan's third season.

During my time, they knew

the ball was coming into me

and they would put two and

three guys in that position before

the ball ever came to me.

I would love to play right now.

I honestly think if I played

right now versus my time,

I'd average 70, 75 points a game.

Wilt Chamberlain

The art of defense is really

an art based on hard work.

Scouting the offense of the

other team emotionally,

intellectually and physically.

Knowing things about the

character or personality

of the opposition. Just knowing

is not sufficient. The defensive

players have to be great

athletes also.

Bill Russell

They embodied the most enduring universal truth in the history of mankind. I don't care what religion you are or what you believe in. It doesn't matter whether you're Catholic, Protestant or Jewish, or whether you read the Talmud, the Confucian Analex or the Koran. You can only receive what you're willing to give. And Magic Johnson and Larry Bird were two of the greatest playmakers and two of the most unselfish players in the history of the game. Not only were they gifted, but they knew what it took to win. They made a habit out of being unselfish. They taught a lot of players what

it is to sacrifice and how and why to think team first and team last. It's not a coincidence that although the NBA may have been at an all-time low in terms of recognition at the time, the league became the sport of the 1980s and today is one of the most popular sports in the world. They brought an incredible desire to win and they realized those desires by making other players better and being unselfish. And they'll go down in history as a result of that.

Pat Riley's nine years as head coach of the Los Angeles Lakers produced seven Finals appearances and four titles.

One of the NBA's greatest rivalries was born in early April, 1979, when Larry Bird's Indiana State team met Earvin Johnson's Michigan State Spartans in the NCAA title game. A year later, Johnson helped the Los Angeles Lakers to the 1980 NBA title with a remarkable Game 6 performance against Philadelphia. The game was shown tape-delayed, and Johnson, too excited to sleep, returned to his hotel and watched the rerun. A year later, Bird's Boston Celtics won the championship. The next season Johnson's Lakers were back in the Finals. By 1984, the first of three memorable championship battles between Bird and Johnson, the NBA Finals were shown live on national television. And by 1987, the last meeting between those two legends, the Finals were beamed to 27 countries around the world.

The L.A. crowd was very laid back. In the fourth quarter, a lot of times you would see people starting to leave because everybody wanted to be seen. It was a fashion show out there. But when the Celtics played in Los Angeles during the 1984 Finals, everybody from the Jacksons to Jack Nicholson to Dyan Cannon became a basketball fan. We

enjoyed going into L.A. with 18,000 or 19,000 people in the stands and putting it to all of them, Magic, Worthy and Byron Scott. And all those guys enjoyed doing the same thing coming into Boston Garden.

Cedric "Cornbread" Maxwell, MVP of the 1984 Finals, played eight of his eleven seasons for Boston.

When a game was coming up, two, three weeks out, people were prepared, man, in both cities. When we hit town it was like the devil hitting town. You'd hear it from the baggage guys at the airport. 'Magic, Larry is going to kill you tomorrow. There's no Magic here! This is Larry's town.' And here comes a guy with his sleeves rolled up, you know he's got the cigarettes right there and he comes over and says, 'Larry's going to do you in, Magic.' I mean, you had to wait for the baggage because in those days there were no private planes.

So you had to walk right through the airport and take all this abuse. And in Boston you had to walk a long way so the ice cream man, the cookie person, everybody got in on it. And you could hear all the whispers, 'Here they come! Here comes the enemy!' Now you had to get on the bus and go through the tunnel. Cab drivers would be beeping their horns around the bus. It was so intense. And when they came to L.A. the same thing happened to them.

Earvin "Magic" Johnson

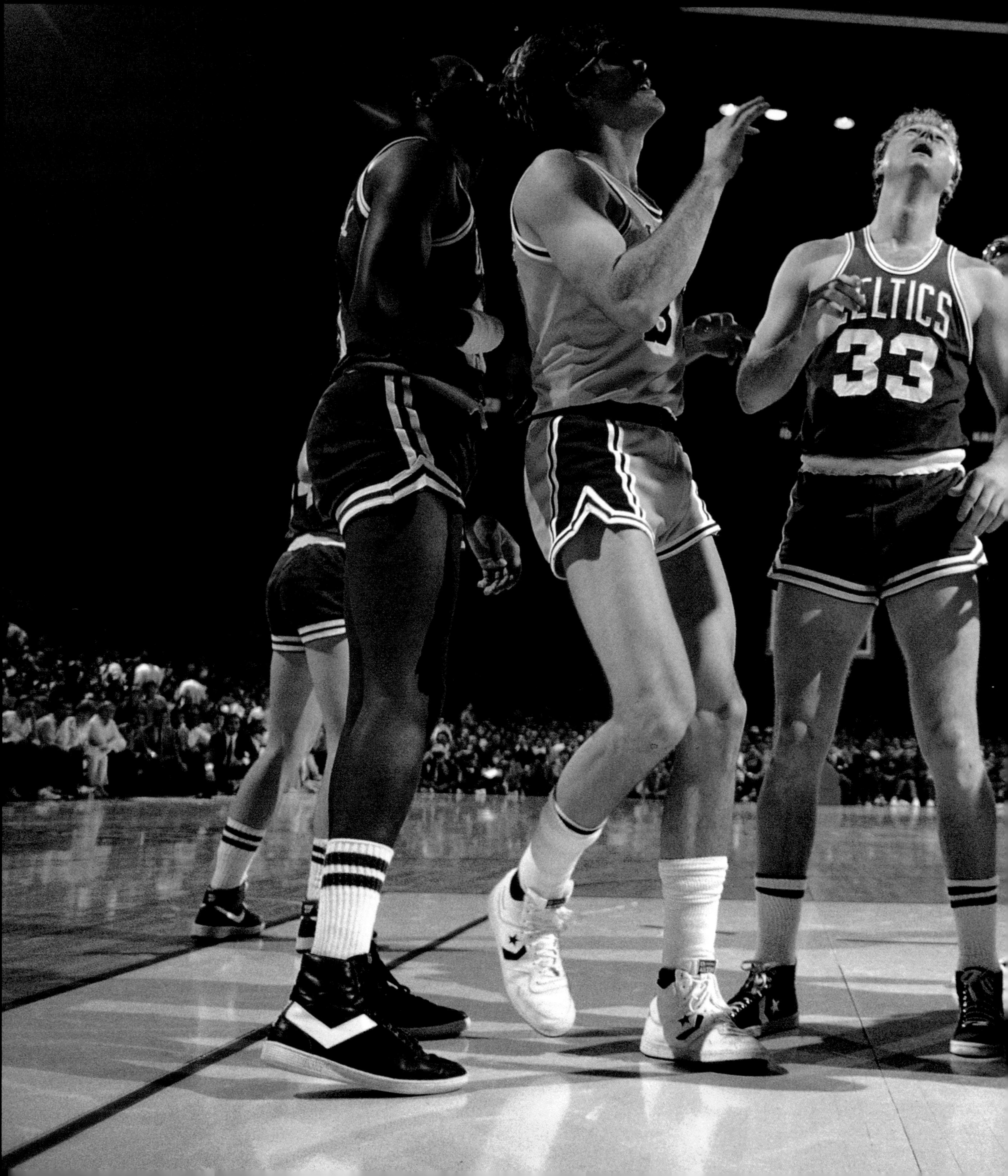
ELTICS
33

1996 NBA DRAFT

AT&T   **IBM**   **Schick**

1	A. IVERSON	9	S. WALKER	16	T. DELK	23	E. RENTZIAS
2	M. CAMBY	10	E. DAMPIER	17	J. O'NEAL	24	D. FISHER
3	S. ABDUR–RAHIM	11	T. FULLER	18	J. WALLACE	25	M. MUURSEPP
4	S. MARBURY	12	V. POTAPENKO	19	W. McCARTY	26	J. WILLIAMS
5	R. ALLEN	13	K. BRYANT	20	Z. ILGAUSKAS	27	B. EVANS
6	A. WALKER	14	P. STOJAKOVIC	21	D. JONES	28	P. LAUDERDALE
7	L. WRIGHT	15	S. NASH	22	R. ROGERS	29	T. KNIGHT
8	K. KITTLES						

In the early years, the draft was used to help franchises develop a local following. So teams were allowed to choose a player who had played college ball in the area before the regular draft. The cost of taking a local hero was the team's first-round draft pick.

As a result, Oscar Robertson, a college star at the University of Cincinnati, ended up playing professionally for the Cincinnati Royals.

The concept was dropped after 1965. However, consider some of the ramifications if that rule had stayed in effect. Magic Johnson would have been a Detroit Piston, Larry Bird an Indiana Pacer and Grant Hill a Charlotte Hornet.

I graduated in 1950 and, believe it or not, I had never seen a professional game. So, obviously, it was not the dream of every kid playing at that time to go on to fame and glory and financial independence in the NBA. I was drafted and someone called me and said, 'Cooz, congratulations, you're the number one pick of the Tri-City Blackhawks.' Gee, I was a pretty good student at Holy Cross, but I must have been asleep in geography. Where the hell is Tri-Cities? That didn't endear me to the good folks of the Tri-Cities. But evidently the owner, Ben Kerner, didn't know where it was either because he lived in Buffalo. And that's where I went to negotiate. I had rolled out of my dorm at Holy Cross, gotten married and opened up an auto driving school at a gas station. I asked him for $10,000 and he offered me $6,000. And I said, 'Gee, thank you very much Mr. Kerner, but I think I'll do something else for a living. And he thought I was bluffing. I taught ladies to drive for the next three months and, frankly, I didn't consider the NBA. I was eventually picked out of a hat after my rights were traded to the Chicago Stags and they folded. They distributed all the players and three of us were left. Our names went into a hat and Boston, which is the only place I was going to play, selected me. I found out when someone called me again and said, 'Hey, Cooz, guess what, Boston picked you out of a hat.' I went down and talked to the owner for five minutes, settled on $9,000. And so, this was not a lifelong dream. I think I pretty much reflected what all the guys felt coming out of school in those days. It just wasn't a big deal.

Bob Cousy played in 13 straight All-Star Games from 1951 through 1963.

From 1966 through 1984 the first pick in the Draft was determined by a coin flip between the teams with the worst record from each conference or division.

At least four of these flips changed the course of NBA history. In 1969 Milwaukee won the toss with Phoenix and selected Kareem Abdul-Jabbar. The Suns ended up with Neal Walk, a solid but unspectacular player. In 1974, Portland landed Bill Walton after winning a toss with Philadelphia, which took Marvin Barnes, who signed with the ABA.

But the last two might have produced the most dramatic short- and long-term effects. In 1979 the Chicago Bulls flipped with the Los Angeles Lakers. The Lakers won and took Earvin "Magic" Johnson and the Bulls selected David Greenwood. Then, in 1984, Houston and Portland, both looking for a center, flipped for the top spot. The Rockets won the flip and took Hakeem Olajuwon while Sam Bowie, solid but often injured, became a Trail Blazer.

The third pick in 1984? Michael Jordan to Chicago.

When my wife Dianne and I accompanied the Atlanta Hawks on an exhibition tour of the then-Soviet Union in 1988, we visited Kaunas, Lithuania, the birthplace of Sarunas Marciulionis and Arvydas Sabonis, who was at the time, the star of the Soviet's National Team. They were proud to show us the gyms where the young Marciulionis and Sabonis had perfected their games, and then they escorted us to the city hall, where we met the mayor, the head of the local Communist Party, and many other dignitaries. After we exchanged pleasantries, the discussion turned to their major concerns, expressed to us through our interpreter: First, wasn't it un-American that the Portland Trail Blazers, who drafted Sabonis in 1986, were the only team with whom Sabonis could negotiate? And, second, did the Blazers have enough room under the salary cap to sign Sabonis?...At that moment, I better understood the global interest in the NBA. Commissioner David Stern

Croatia's Drazen Petrovic, one of the league's greatest shooters during his four-year NBA career, prepares to make a move on Michael Jordan during the 1992 Barcelona Olympics. Petrovic, a superstar in Europe before coming to the NBA, died in an automobile accident prior to the 1993-94 season.

I started playing basketball when I was 17 years old. I had played soccer in Nigeria since I was two or three years old. All my friends said I was too tall for soccer. They said it was better I play basketball. But I didn't know anything about basketball until I met a coach from the Nigerian national team. He was just riding through our neighborhood and he saw me playing soccer. He asked how tall I was. I was about 6-feet-9 then. He asked me,

I said no. He opened his trunk and gave me a basketball and took me to the basketball gym. He showed me examples of how to shoot a lay-up and I couldn't do it. He was trying to show me how to dunk the ball. I couldn't dunk for a couple weeks, but I started getting interested in the game.

Hakeem Olajuwon had played basketball for just eight years when he carried the Houston Rockets to the 1986 NBA Finals.

I was asked by the State Department to get a team and go behind the Iron Curtain in 1964. We met the Secretary of State, we met the President, and every country we went to would have cocktail parties for us. You know, big, big things. It was the first time a professional team had ever worked behind the Iron Curtain. The Russians wouldn't play us because they knew how good we were. But we went to Poland and Yugoslavia. We had K.C. Jones, Tom Gola, Bob Cousy and Oscar Robertson. Then I had Tommy Heinsohn, Bob Pettit, Bill Russell and Jerry Lucas. Those were my eight guys. Normally we would beat them by 30 or 40 points. We would let them know we were decisive winners, but we didn't want to really rub it in. We could have beaten some of those smaller countries by 90 points, but that was never my style anyway. But we had to show the American superiority. So we beat them by 36 in the first game. And these guys were big. They were tough and they could play. So that night they had a banquet for us. The home team doesn't show. We were in the middle of this Cold War crap. So I got mad. Before this whole thing started I had insisted that before we played a game, the American flag had to be hung. The American Embassy said we can't do that. Bull! If you can't, I can. Anyway, they put it up. Now I'm mad. So before the second game I said, '50 points.' The game was rough, really rough. So I call their guy over and I get a guy to translate. Before I can say a word, the guy is screaming. He said, 'We're mad at your team because yesterday you didn't line your players on the foul line and bow to the crowd.' I said, 'Those people were booing and whistling at us. They weren't nice. No goddamn way! Furthermore, you tell that guy that if he doesn't tell his players to play ball instead of seeing how tough they are, we're going to do two things: One, we're going to beat you so bad, you're going to want to quit the game. And the other thing is we're going to beat the hell out of you.' So we finished the game and won by 58. That night we had another party. They all showed up. The ice was broken. They wanted autographs. They asked me, 'How do you think we'd do against the American amateurs?'

Red Auerbach. In 1989 Auerbach's Boston Celtics drafted Croatia's Dina Radja in the second round of the NBA Draft.

Playing against the Dream Team in 1992 was like being on the same stage as the Beatles. It seemed that most of the teams did not think of themselves as opponents. They thought of themselves as part of the show. It was sort of like a great musician who was asked to be a backup to John, Paul, George and Ringo. One guy was guarding Magic Johnson and, during the game, he kept asking if he could have Magic's jersey after the game. For them, it was a dream come true just to be on the same court with the greatest players in the world.

Russ Granik is Deputy Commissioner of the NBA and a Vice President of USA Basketball.

By 1987 the decade-long dominance of Boston and Los Angeles had begun to show its age. Boston barely survived a grueling seven-game series with Detroit in the Eastern Conference Finals, ironically saved only by a remarkable defensive play by Larry Bird. A year later, the defensive-minded Pistons closed the door on Boston's Bird Era by knocking off the Celtics before taking the defending champion Lakers to a seventh game in the Finals. Then, in 1989, Detroit dispatched Los Angeles just as it had Boston, sweeping the Lakers 4-0 for the first of two consecutive NBA titles.

When we lost to Boston in Game 7 in 1987, that prepared us to get to the Finals the next year. Then getting to the Finals in 1988 prepared us for winning in 1989. When you suffer something like that defeat to the Celtics, as an individual you go through the summer reliving that every day. And one of two things is going to happen. You are going to learn from that experience or you're going to crumble beneath the memory. We had the right kind of character to not give up. We were going to fight to do whatever we had to do to win a championship. These things prepared us to be champions.

Detroit Pistons guard Joe Dumars was the Most Valuable Player of the 1989 Finals, scoring 17 consecutive points during one stretch in Game 3.

Few teams in history have been more resilient than the Houston Rockets were during back-to-back title runs in 1994 and 1995.

Seven times the Rockets faced an elimination game and seven times they came back to win the series.

In 1995, Houston became the first team to eliminate four teams that had won 50 or more games during the regular season. They fell behind 2-1 in the first round to the Utah Jazz, then 3-1 in the Western Conference Semifinals against the Phoenix Suns. Both times they came back.

Houston joined Boston, Detroit, the Lakers (includes Minneapolis and Los Angeles) and Chicago as the only franchises to win back-to-back titles while Olajuwon joined Michael Jordan as the only players to be named Finals' MVP in consecutive years. Olajuwon averaged 33.0 points, 10.3 rebounds and more than five assists throughout the playoffs.

One of the biggest thrills of my basketball career has been the experience of being around Hakeem Olajuwon. He's just an amazing player. The performance he put on during the playoffs for our second championship is the most consistent run of great games I have ever seen. Here he was against San Antonio, playing against a great player in David Robinson, and Hakeem was just in a different zone. He had all the coaches looking at one another in amazement.

Rudy Tomjanovich was a five-time All-Star during his ten years with the Rockets. He became head coach in 1992.

I never planned on coaching being a career. It's just something that happened. But none of us coaches ever thought anyone would approach Red's record. It's something we never even thought about. Then all of a sudden people started talking about how I had the best opportunity. Red is someone I've always respected. I've always thought he used personnel as well as anyone I've ever seen in the game of basketball. When I realized he had been pulling for me, that made it special. I lit the cigar in his honor. I'd never smoked a cigarette or a cigar, or anything for that matter. I almost choked to death. But I felt like I wanted to

Lenny Wilkens

make a little tribute to him,

so I lit one up

Lenny Wilkens surpassed Red Auerbach's victory total of 938 on January 6, 1995, and won his 1000th regular-season game during the 1995-96 season.

Chicago put together one of the most dominating postseason performances in NBA history in 1991. The Bulls swept New York 3-0 in the first round, winning by an average of 20 points. Philadelphia fell in five games, 4-1, in the Eastern Conference Semifinals by an average of 11 points. Two-time defending champion Detroit bowed in four straight by an average of 11.5 points in the Conference Finals and the Los Angeles Lakers, after winning Game 1 in Chicago, lost four straight by an average of 12.7 points as the Bulls finished 15-2.

Chicago's 67-15 regular season record in 1991-92 was the NBA's third-best mark at that time. Its 10.4 point differential was the highest since the 1971-72 Lakers' 12.3 and the Milwaukee Bucks' 11.1 the same year.

The Bulls third straight title made them only the third franchise in NBA history to win as many championships consecutively and the first since the Boston Celtics of the 1960s. Nine players from Chicago's first title team remained, including Michael Jordan, Scottie Pippen, Horace Grant, Bill Cartwright, John Paxson, Scott Williams, Will Perdue, B.J. Armstrong and Stacey King.

The best team I ever saw was the 1967 76ers team. There were ten teams in the league then and we're going up against Boston, the defending champion, nine or ten times a year. Now, win half your games against the good teams and you've got 70 wins. Everything is geared for the offensive players. Open the middle so he can drive. You can't put a hand on a guy's back. Can you imagine me in the paint with only one guy on me and he can't put his hands on me? Jordan — he's not going to come through dunking against Luke Jackson. He's going to get slammed to the floor. I'd like to see Wali Jones playing defense on him, driving him into me. I'd be more than happy to see that.

Wilt Chamberlain's playoff numbers in 1967: 21.7 points, 29.1 rebounds, 9.0 assists, 47.9 minutes per game.

EVERYTHING SEEMED TO GO PERFECTLY. It was an opening in the clouds. There were no injuries at all. I was definitely at the twilight of my career and I certainly couldn't play the game the way I had before. It just seemed that everything, from Day 1 in training camp, worked nicely. Our players were at the age of their careers where everything would be concentrated on the team and not on individual things. It was an almost perfect season. You didn't have to think for anyone.

Everyone thought collectively. Jerry West on the 1971-72 Los Angeles Lakers.

How good were the 1966-67 76ers?

- Wilt Chamberlain finished third in the league in scoring (24.1), first in field-goal percentage (.683), third in assists (7.8) and first in rebounds (24.2).

- They beat Boston and Bill Russell 4-1 in the Eastern Division Finals winning by an average of 13.5 points.

- Billy Cunningham, one of four Hall of Famers on the team, came off the bench.

- Until the 76ers won 68, no team had ever won more than 62 and no team had come close to their .840 winning percentage.

- The 9.4 point differential was the highest since the NBA's first season. Only one of Boston's 11 championship teams ever had a differential of even nine points.

How good were the 1971-72 Lakers?

- The Lakers 33-game winning streak is the longest in NBA history by 13 games, or more than 39%.

- Their 12.3 regular-season point differential is the highest in NBA history.

- Hall of Fame guards Gail Goodrich and Jerry West remain the most prolific backcourt tandem in history, averaging 25.9 and 25.8 points per game, respectively.

- The Lakers went 69-13 during the regular season and 12-3 in the Playoffs.

- Until the Lakers went 31-7 on the road, no team had won as many as 29 road games.

I think we would have beaten the Bulls. That team doesn't have anybody that could match up with Moses Malone. Besides, the league was tougher with Magic's Lakers, Larry Bird's Celtics. Chicago didn't have an equal, much less a Boston, during the 1995-96 regular season.

Julius Erving's Philadelphia 76ers teams went to the
Finals four times in six seasons between 1977 and 1983.

**How good were the
1985-86 Celtics?**

• Hall of Fame front line of Larry Bird,
  Robert Parish and Kevin McHale
  averaged better than 6-10.

• They went 9-0 against other three
  division winners, 15-3 in playoffs.

• Celtics 9.4 point differential was
  the highest in franchise history.

• Bill Walton had 106 blocks and
  averaged 6.8 rebounds off the bench.

• McHale and Dennis Johnson were
  named to the All-Defensive First Team.

We were a big team with a lot of weapons.
It would have been difficult for any team to
match up with our front line. And with Bill
coming off the bench we always had a presence.

Larry Bird won three consecutive MVP awards and his Boston Celtics
made three consecutive Finals appearances from 1984-86.

**How good were the
1982-83 76ers?**

• The team finished 67-15 despite
  injuries to starters Julius Erving
  (missed 10 games), Bobby Jones
  (8) and Moses Malone (4).

• They went 12-1 in the playoffs,
  for a record .923 winning
  percentage.

• They beat the defending champion Los Angeles Lakers four
  straight in the Finals by an
  average of 10 points a game.

• They led the league in rebounds
  and blocked shots.

• Malone averaged just over
  37 minutes a game; no other
  player averaged as many as 34.

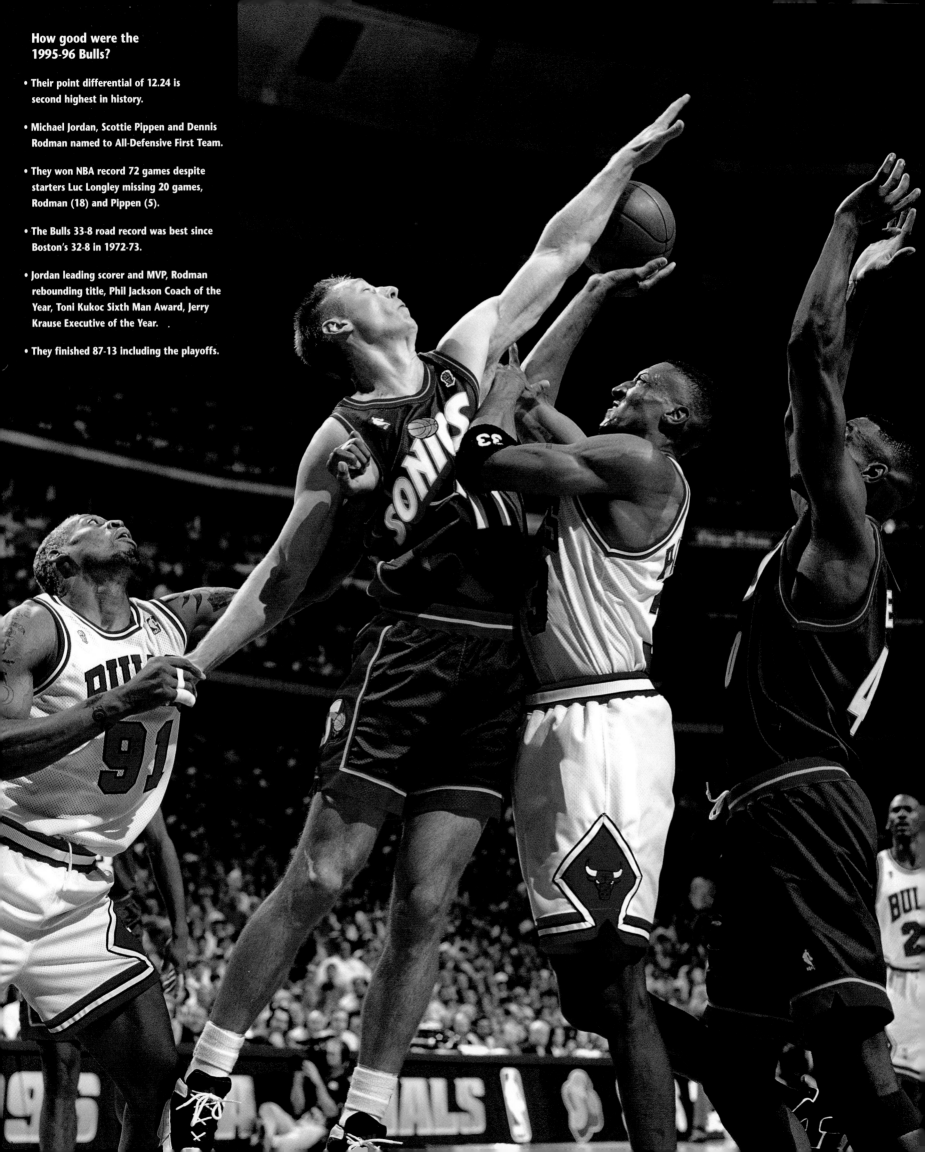

How good were the 1995-96 Bulls?

- Their point differential of 12.24 is second highest in history.

- Michael Jordan, Scottie Pippen and Dennis Rodman named to All-Defensive First Team.

- They won NBA record 72 games despite starters Luc Longley missing 20 games, Rodman (18) and Pippen (5).

- The Bulls 33-8 road record was best since Boston's 32-8 in 1972-73.

- Jordan leading scorer and MVP, Rodman rebounding title, Phil Jackson Coach of the Year, Toni Kukoc Sixth Man Award, Jerry Krause Executive of the Year.

- They finished 87-13 including the playoffs.

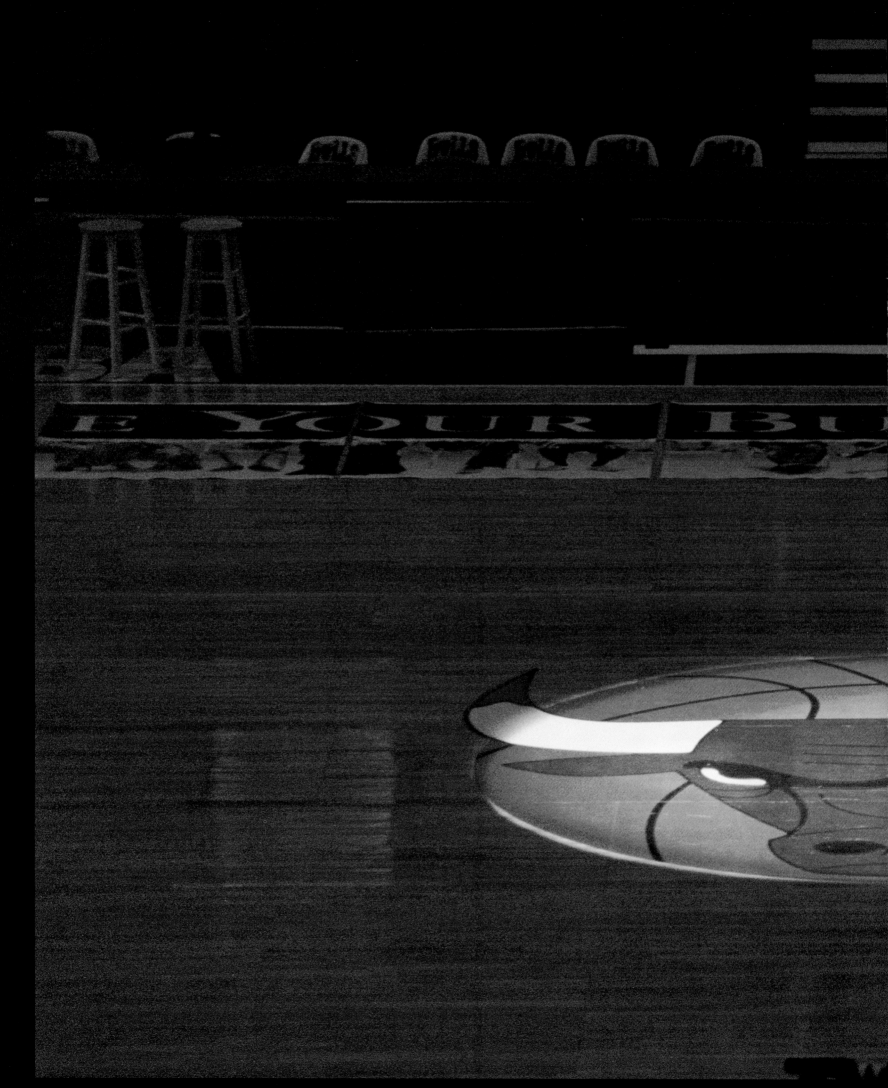

Anybody else win 72 games? Michael Jordan

You weren't
making a lot of
money in the 1960s,
so in most cases
guys had to find
jobs in the off-
season. You couldn't
sit back and live
off the income
you made playing
professional
basketball.
Many players
started their next
careers early by
working a few
months after
the season
selling real estate,
working at a bank,
jobs that would
prepare them for
the end of their
playing careers.
In those days
you could play for
maybe six or seven
years before you
had to stop
and find work.

Billy Cunningham

THE LIGHTS
GO DOWN

Hard work, intelligence and discipline are the key ingredients of anyone's success. With them, a person of any color can overcome practical

y obstacle — and that includes discrimination, poverty, and almost any other condition that has nothing to do with your will to succeed.

Charles Barkley

When the NBA conducted a series of basketball clinics in Africa in 1993, we visited a refugee camp near the Kenya-Somalia border. They told us

before we got there that as many as 1▮▮ people a day were dying from starvation in Somalia. We went to visit a school and they brought a

group to entertain us. I looked at them when they came in, and **three of the little boys had on Chicago Bulls tee shirts** with Michael Jordan's number 23 on them. The tee shirts

were torn, but they were the most prized possessions those kids had.

Wes Unseld was elected to the Naismith Memorial Basketball Hall of Fame in 1987.

**When basketball is spoken, no translation is needed.
It has become an independent international language.**

Commissioner David Stern

Seattle SuperSonics All-Star forward Shawn Kemp spends some downtime flinging fish at Seattle's Pike Place Market.

Kareem Abdul-Jabbar at home.

Kareem was an interesting guy because he changed his name from Lew Alcindor. He became a Muslim and that was a period in his life where there was a lot of controversial stuff happening around him. He was different.

He brought a different mentality into the game as a person, different from what we had seen before,

kind of like Dennis Rodman is bringing something different to the game, something the game has never seen before. So Kareem had that same kind of attitude. He brought his Muslim faith. At that time the Muslim religion was not totally accepted by society. He was so much into his faith that I think that was one of the reasons he was a little distant. But he's a good guy, a nice person and a good friend.

Chet "The Jet" Walker was an All-Star seven times and scored 18,831 points during his 13 seasons from 1962 through 1974-75.

My religion is Islam and it's a way of life. There is no separation between my faith and my work. It requires you to strive to be the best you can be. My motivation is not that I want to be the best, because my religion teaches that it is your duty to maximize your God-given talent. It teaches you the discipline that is necessary for sports.

Ramadan is one of the pillars of Islam. Fasting is prescribed for you as it was prescribed for people before you so that you will learn self-control. It is a pillar of the faith that you cannot compromise. You have to get up at 4:30 to eat your breakfast. At that time in the morning, you can't really eat anything heavy. It's too early for that. After that, you won't eat or drink until sunset. Ramadan is not just about food. It is about concentration. It is where you feel closer to God and you try to be more righteous, more devoted. So your concentration level is very high. The first three days are very difficult because you shock your body. After three days, it becomes much easier. People think, and I used to think, it was almost impossible. But food is sometimes heavy and it can slow you down. I realized that when I fasted, it really made me better because I'm not as full and I am faster and quicker.   Hakeem Olajuwon

Growing up as a little boy I always dreamed of owning my own 18-wheeler. I remember riding with my mom and seeing 'em on the road and telling her, 'I'm going to own one of them some day.' Being out on the road, there's a power to it. There's a smell to it — a clean diesel truck — that gives it a kind of aura. It's a power-kind of feeling. **People think athletes aren't supposed to do anything that's a little different.** But, hey, this makes me happy. Maybe it is weird. But it's me. I love cattle and I love westerns. So, on one side, I have cowboys herding cattle. On the other side, it's nighttime and the cowboys are gathered around a campfire with a thunderstorm rolling in. People ask me, **'Did they just give the license to you because you're Karl Malone?'** But they didn't. I studied my butt off and watched hours of film. Then I went down and took the test. I did it myself. They didn't give it to me, I can tell you that. I have a lot of interests, like ranching, trucking and fishing and my family.

Karl Malone's trucking firm now consists of his personal 18-wheeler.
In addition to his working ranch in El Dorado, Arkansas, Malone and
Utah Jazz owner Larry H. Miller own a Toyota dealership in Albuquerque.

My job has never been playing basketball. My job starts the minute I step off the court. Michael Jordan

he has become something of a 24-hour commodity.

The biggest challenge for the new NBA star

is, one, keeping his head together and being consistently productive. And then, carrying the mantle that's been left by players such as Magic, Larry Bird, Charles Barkley, Michael Jordan, Karl Malone, John Stockton, Patrick Ewing and all the other great players. Everyone knows who those people are. They established a level of professionalism that I think young players should strive to meet.

Lenny Wilkens